Introducing
Relational Database

Alan Mayne
Michael B Wood

PUBLISHED BY NCC PUBLICATIONS

British Library Cataloguing in Publication Data

Mayne, Alan
   Introducing relational database.
   1. Electronic data processing – Relational processing
   I. Title   II. Wood, Michael B.
001.64'42   QA76.9.R/

ISBN 0-85012-397-6

First published in 1983 by:

NCC Publications, The National Computing Centre Limited, Oxford Road, Manchester M1 7ED, England.

Typeset by UPS Blackburn Limited, 76-80 Northgate, Blackburn, Lancashire, and printed by Hobbs the Printers of Southampton.

ISBN 0-85012-397-6

Acknowledgements

Relational database depends upon the sound foundation of the pioneering work of Dr E F Codd of IBM. The present authors acknowledge their debt to him and to other workers, particularly C J Date. The literature on relational systems is extensive. A short reading list appears at the end of the book. Much of the literature is difficult for the non-mathematical reader.

The authors also thank the various suppliers for their help with information, and for their valuable comments on certain parts of the draft. In many cases we have simplified explanations and omitted details in the interest of clarity. Again the reader should consult suppliers for current product information.

Our thanks also to Rosemary Wood who read and criticised the MS and to Geoff Simons who gave much help as Editor.

The Centre acknowledges with thanks the support of the Electronics and Avionics Requirements Board for the project from which this book derives.

Prologue

A dynamic young sales executive decided to give up his expense account and become an entrepreneur. It was fashionable, and politicians encouraged the notion that small business start-ups would save the country.

At first our entrepreneur was in total control of his new business. All the information was at his finger tips or in his head. He had a compact and efficient filing system for his data; in fact he had a database: *A database is a collection of stored data organised in such a way that all user data requirements are satisfied by the database. In general there is only one logical copy of each item of data.*

Our entrepreneur's business is small. He only keeps one record of each item of data, because he has no time to do more.

The business expands rapidly until there are several departments, and branch offices. Our entrepreneur can no longer exercise complete control, but must rely upon his managers.

The various managers need data to control their own areas, so each builds his own set of files and ledgers. Ideally they would have shared a common set of data, and used similar systems, but this is not an ideal world. Some managers did know that others were collecting and using the same, or similar data. Some did not care even when they knew. Some managers did not trust the data from others, and would not risk becoming dependent for political reasons. No manager wanted to share his hard-won data with others, because the data might have been used against him in the struggle to the top.

How had success affected the company? When it was a one-man show the data needed to run it was available from one source. Duplication of data was rare. The company could indeed claim to have a database. However, the company's expansion resulted in data being spread around and there was considerable duplication of data.

No one knew what data was actually being maintained across the company. Managers were blissfully ignorant of the problems created by duplication of data. More correctly, they were ignorant of the cause and attributed the problems to the incompetence of others.

If the address of a customer changed, the information was usually only sent to one department in the company. The department lucky enough to receive the notification could ensure that goods and correspondence were sent to the new correct address. However, other departments would continue to use the old address, being unaware of the change.

The company demonstrated to its customers that its left hand did not know what its right hand was doing. The problem arose because the company held multiple copies of essentially the same items of data which became inconsistent as individual copies were modified. Departmental managers were using out-of-date and inaccurate data to make their decisions. Clearly, this was not the right way to run the business!

Our entrepreneur was now a worried man. He received inconsistent and conflicting reports from his departmental managers, and could not plan the company's future.

One day a computer salesman walked into his office. The computer salesman listened patiently to our entrepreneur's problems as they enjoyed an expense-account lunch. (The salesman had heard it all before, many many times.) The salesman explained how all the problems would be solved by the magic of computers. After making the sale he rushed off to order a new car.

The company created a data processing department, hiring teams of expensive programmers and analysts from outside. Analysts designed elaborate computerised systems to meet the perceived requirements of the various departments. In practice, the managers had found it very difficult to specify precisely what they wanted. Eventually, after many months of development, the data processing department provided an acceptable, though imperfect, system.

The computer processed large volumes of data faster and more reliably than had ever been possible with clerical methods. However, our entrepreneur still encountered difficulty in getting consistent and accurate reports from his departmental managers. There were still some problems from inconsistent data. (One department refused a customer's business because his credit limit had been exceeded. At the same time another department sent letters to the same customer saying how glad they were to have his business.)

The black box in the computer room failed to solve the original problems. Worse than this, it introduced many new ones.

Departmental managers now complained about the cost and time it took to make apparently trivial changes to these computerised systems. The data processing department told them that they would have to wait months to get an extra piece of data printed on one small report. Moreover they told them that it would cost them several thousand pounds for program modifications.

The data processing manager explained to our entrepreneur why maintenance took so long and was so very costly. In order to print the extra data on the report it was necessary to change the format of the computer files to accommodate the new data. In consequence, every one of the computer programs that used the modified computer file also had to be altered, not only the single report program. This meant that 37 programs were affected by the change, not just one. The programs were unfortunately dependent upon the data, even upon data that they did not actually use.

Our entrepreneur called in the computer salesman once more. He told him of the new problems created by the computer. He also pointed out that it had done little to resolve the original problems. The salesman was unabashed by these remarks. He claimed to understand the problem completely. Indeed he had the perfect solution. The company should "go database".

The salesman explained the benefits of going database. The company's data would be stored on the computer in a way which would allow everyone's requirements to be satisfied. Everyone would share the same data. There would be only one copy of each item of data so all those headaches caused by duplicate data would be solved.

The salesman also explained that to "go database" the company needed to buy a database management system (DBMS). In addition to supporting a database the salesman pointed out that the DBMS software also provided data independence. This allows new data to be added to support a new program without requiring any existing programs to be modified. It also supported back-up and recovery facilities as well as access control facilities. A Database Management System is formally defined as:

> a general-purpose set of programs that aid and control each user's access to and use of the database for adding, modifying and retrieving data, and that includes facilities for giving data independence, integrity and security.

The sales talk was convincing and the entrepreneur signed the contract and instructed the data processing manager to start using the DBMS to implement new systems. He then waited for the promised benefits of "going database".

Alas not all the benefits were forthcoming. The old problems refused to disappear. Managers still provided him with conflicting reports. The difficulties caused by data duplication persisted. On the positive side though, the DBMS had eased the problems of program maintenance. The integrity and security facilities also proved useful.

Our entrepreneur then called in a Data Management Consultant to find out what had gone wrong. The consultant listened sympathetically. He had heard this story many times before; to him it was like being a marriage guidance counsellor listening to a wife telling of her husband's affairs. After hearing the story and studying the organisation of the company, he explained what had gone wrong and suggested what needed to be done to put things right.

When the company was a one-man show it could claim to have a database, although not a computer-based one. The growth of the company destroyed the database. It was replaced by a collection of filing systems that were not integrated, and had considerable duplication of data. Introducing the computer in no way changed the company's attitude to data. The computerised systems simply replaced manual files with computerised files. Each department still maintained its own set of files for its own computer systems. There was no integration of data among the various departments.

When the company decided to "go database" there was hope that the problems might be resolved. The company did not know what "going database" really meant, and it merely introduced a database management system. The DBMS continued to model the fragmentation that actually existed. Each department continued to have its own copy of the data it needed. The DBMS was simply being used as an access method. Use of a DBMS does not automatically mean that a database exists.

The root of the company's problems was that technical tools were being introduced, first the computer, then the DBMS, in an attempt to solve managerial problems. The real problem was the company's attitude to its own data. Irrespective of whether the company's data is stored in filing cabinets, conventional computer files, or under the control of a DBMS, it is essential to have a philosophy of sharing data and eliminating, or at least controlling, duplication of data.

The technical problems of sharing data and controlling duplication can be solved relatively easily. The political problems are often much more intractable. Departmental managers have to understand the need for data sharing. They must appreciate that the data they collect and use belongs to the company as a whole. Senior management must define who shall be responsible for updating specific items of data and also who shall be allowed to access which items of data.

Having a database means having a philosophy of sharing data for the benefit of the entire company. An on-going commitment of senior management is necessary. It is all too easy for a database to degenerate into a collection of unintegrated data files. The state of well-organised data is intrinsically unstable. It needs to be continually policed. For this reason it is usual to establish a Data or Database Administration function to act as the police force.

At this point in our story another salesman arrived at the company. He too listened sympathetically to our entrepreneur's tale of woe. Naturally enough he also had the perfect solution. It was a *relational database system*.

What could he have meant?

Contents

Section 1

CONCEPTS AND FEATURES

1 **Relational Database Concepts**
2 **Relational Languages**
3 **Keys and Normalisation**
4 **Logical Structuring and Data Independence**
5 **Access Control**
6 **Security and Integrity**
7 **Relational Database Technology**

1 Relational Database Concepts

GENERAL

The relational database approach has become extremely popular in the last few years. Upwards of 100 relational products were on offer in the US in the autumn of 1982. The term *relational* has acquired special significance, especially among sales and marketing people.

Data processing exists to help solve problems in business and administration. In data processing we take files of data and process them in various ways to provide *results* to help people to be more effective in an enterprise. Relational systems are important because they give *simplicity and generality* in most kinds of data processing.

Relational systems operate conceptually on whole files or tables of data, rather than on the individual data items within a file. One specifies operations on whole files, so that the treatment is at a much higher level than in other systems. Complex requests for information, perhaps involving several files, can be specified very simply without difficulty or ambiguity. Moreover, relational systems are very easy to use, with very short learning times. They could save people time which is scarce and expensive.

Relational systems have a sound mathematical foundation which provides benefits in area like integrity and recovery. Developments in hardware and software engineering have provided practical implementations after a decade of research work.

The earliest published work on relational systems was a series of papers by Dr E F Codd of IBM in the late 1960s. Many other workers have refined the original concepts, and developed various approaches to the relational ideal. Relational systems have been implemented by research

17

workers, and practical tools now exist. Examples of these are described in Section 2.

TABLES

The fundamental concept in relational systems is the table. The idea of a table is well understood. A table provides a natural mechanism for conveying information in a compact form. It has a number of columns, one for each attribute of the objects or entities described. Each entry in the table is a row containing values for each attribute. Each row can be considered as a *record*, with each column as a field of that record.

A typical example is shown below.

SALESFORCE

Salesman Number	Name	Sales Area	Target
01	JONES	LONDON	20000
02	SMITH	PARIS	25000
03	BROWN	EDINBURGH	15000
04	STEVENS	SWEDEN	40000
05	HARRIS	GLASGOW	10000
06	KING	NEW YORK	25000

This table has typical structure. There are four columns each with a heading: Salesman Number, Name, Sales Area, Target. These column headings form part of the table. Without them the table is much less useful. For instance who could guess what the fourth column represents, without the heading?

The table has six entries represented by the six rows. Each row corresponds to one member of the salesforce. If the salesforce had more people, the table would have more rows.

Such tables are very common in data processing. The table is convenient and easily understood. A practical table could have very many rows, and there might be many more columns.

In mathematics, a structure like a table can be treated as a *relation*. If certain conditions are satisfied mathematical relational theory can be applied. This results in a uniform and consistent approach, called the relational approach.

Is a relational database system then simply one that handles tables? No. There are a number of relatively simple rules that must be satisfied if the database system is to qualify as a relational one. (A database system that handles tables is not necessarily a relational one, despite the claims of some vendors.)

The rules are derived from the underlying mathematical theory, which provides a sound theoretical foundation. This gives practical benefits in areas like integrity and recovery as we shall see in later chapters. The basic rules are as follows:

— within a relational system the table must contain only one type of record. Each record has a fixed number of fields, all of which are explicitly named. The database will usually contain numerous tables, so that different kinds of records are held in different tables;

— within a table the fields are distinct, and repeating groups are not allowed;

— each record within a table is unique; there are no duplicate records;

— the order of the records within the table is indeterminate. The records may come in any order, and there is no predetermined sequence;

— the fields within any column take their values from a *domain* of possible field values. (The idea of a domain and its use in relational systems is explained below.) The same domain can be used for many different field types, perhaps in several tables;

— finally, new tables can be produced on the basis of a match of field values from the same domain in two existing tables. The formation of new tables from existing tables is the essence of relational processing.

Let us examine these ideas in more detail. The database contains a number of tables. It is these *tables* that are processed by the relational database system. The results of the processing are new tables. Notice that the operations are on whole tables, rather than on the individual records in the tables. We are considering something much more powerful than record-by-record processing characteristic of other systems.

The rules about the fields and records in the tables are necessary if the underlying mathematical theory is to be used. The theoretical basis allows development of a satisfactory system where results are predictable.

The tables in a relational system must be rectangular, with the same number of elements in each row. Repeating groups are not allowed, but this can usually be overcome by simply using more records or rows, or by using more tables.

The idea of a *domain* of possible values is very important. All the values in a column refer to one attribute of the elements represented by the rows in the table. One column could hold a name, another a price, a third might hold a part number, and so on. For consistency, all the values in a column must be drawn from some domain of possible values (of, for example, part number).

The domain is the set of possible values for some attribute. In any particular table not all these possible values need occur. Indeed, this would be most unlikely to happen except in very special cases.

For instance one might define an employee number as a letter followed by three digits, eg A123, T462. The domain for employee number is therefore all possible instances of 'letter digit digit digit' and there are 26000 such instances. We might have details about a few hundred employees represented within a particular relational system. Each employee number would be drawn from the domain just defined. Most of the possible employee numbers in the domain would not be used for the attribute employee number.

Furthermore a number that is not in the domain, such as XY73, would not be a valid employee number. The concept of domain provides powerful means of ensuring valid and meaningful processing in a relational system.

Relational processing often depends upon values within a column of a table, and how these match with specified values elsewhere. If the values in a column represented, say, sterling, it would be meaningless to match these with sales quantities. All the values must be drawn from the same domain if the processing is to have meaning. Relational systems therefore require that all the values in a given column shall be drawn from a common domain of values. Sometimes this domain can or must be specified. In other systems the domain is implicit. We shall explore the idea of domains in a later chapter.

To anyone raised in classical data processing the point about record order is at first sight a very strange one. Within a relational system the order of the records is indeterminate. The operations in the relational system act upon whole tables or sets of records. The order of the records within the set has no significance. The table is simply an unordered set of records. It is processed as a set.

In practice though, many systems do allow the user to specify the order in which rows are presented on output. One or more fields or columns can be chosen as the key, with ascending or descending order. This does not affect the relational processing, merely the output presentation of a table. The processing still acts upon whole tables as a set; it is only the presentation that is affected.

Some relational systems are designed to interface with conventional high-level languages such as COBOL or FORTRAN. The relational database system processes tables, the results being then made available to the host language system. At this stage the information is presented record by record, since the host language cannot usually accept the table as a whole.

The records that form the table then, are an unordered set. The actual fields or attributes within the records are also not in any defined order. They also can be held as a set by the system. Obviously any presentation of the table has some order. There must be *some* attribute at the first printed column, and another in the second. This is however simply an external view. The underlying database table is simply a set of records in one dimension, and a set of attributes in the other dimension. Neither set has any order as a rule.

The items in a relational system *might* be held in some order. If loss of this ordering implies loss of information, then something is missing. Ordering cannot validly form part of the relational system. One or more extra keys should be included as attributes of the individual record. Keys are an important aspect of the relational approach, as we shall see.

Having looked briefly at the data, let us look at some of the processing facilities of relational systems.

RELATIONAL OPERATIONS

The fundamental relational operations are: – *selection* (which creates a subset of all the rows in a table); – *projection* (which creates a subset of the columns of a table); – *join* (which combines two tables). The result of these operations is always a new table.

Selection

This is the simplest operation. It selects certain rows from the table. The original table is processed to produce a new table, using some selection criteria to pick certain rows from the original table. These are used to build the new table. (One typical criterion could be that one or more fields have a specific value.) All rows that satisfy the criteria are selected for the new table. The new table will have some, all, or possibly none, of the rows from the original table. The result clearly depends upon the values of the fields involved in the selection criteria. Notice also that the operation acts upon one table to produce another one 'at one fell swoop'.

Selection could be illustrated with the following table:

SALESFORCE

Salesman Number	Name	Sales Area	Target
01	JONES	LONDON	20000
02	SMITH	PARIS	25000
03	BROWN	EDINBURGH	15000
04	STEVENS	SWEDEN	40000
05	HARRIS	GLASGOW	10000
06	KING	NEW YORK	25000

We could select records with target 15000 or less to produce a new table:

LOW TARGET

Salesman Number	Name	Sales Area	Target
03	BROWN	EDINBURGH	15000
05	HARRIS	GLASGOW	10000

The result of the selection is a new table. The order of the records in the new table is indeterminate, so that in our illustration the two records could have been presented in either order.

If the selection criterion had been 'target less than 50000', then the new table would have all the records from the old one. On the other hand, 'target less than 5000' would have given an empty result. So the new table can contain all, some or none of the original set of records.

Projection

Here certain columns are selected from the original table to produce a new table. The new table thus contains only some of the original columns, the rest being ignored. Selection acts on the rows, projection on the columns. In the resulting table thus projected there might be some duplicate records, because two records from the original table might have differed only on columns that have been eliminated in the projection. Duplicate records are not allowed in a relational table, so only one of such records is retained. The result of a projection usually contains fewer columns than the original table. (Projection on all columns would copy the table.) It will often contain fewer rows than the original table, because duplicate rows will normally be eliminated. Some implementations allow duplicates, others make it optional.

The projection operation could be used on the table SALESFORCE to produce target information. We could project the Name and Target to produce:

TARGETS

Name	Target
JONES	20000
SMITH	25000
BROWN	15000
STEVENS	40000
HARRIS	10000
KING	25000

The new table has six records but only two columns projected from the original table SALESFORCE. Usually the columns can be projected in any order into the new table.

We could project the column Target from either table to produce a new table TARGET-VALUES:

TARGET VALUES

Target
20000
25000
15000
40000
10000

Notice that the new table has only five entries. The duplicate 25000 value is eliminated, as part of the operation.

Systems usually allow selection and projection to be combined in one request. We can therefore select certain rows from the original table, and project only certain columns. The combination of the two operations allows one to select from a table both the records and the fields from those records to satisfy some enquiry. Of course, the information in the resulting table comes from one original table.

Join

Often one needs to combine information from different tables. The relational operation for this is the *join*, which creates a new table from two existing tables. There are several kinds of join. The *natural* join is the most usual.

The join is done by matching the values occurring in a pair of columns, one from each table. The two columns would usually represent some similar attribute, such as 'employee number'. The values for the matching pair of attributes would be drawn from the same domain. The *join* operation produces a new table containing records formed by joining (concatenating) records from the two original tables. Typically there is one new record for every matching pair of values from the original tables.

We might take the table SALESFORCE and join it with another table
CUSTOMERS:

SALESFORCE

Salesman Number	Name	Sales Area	Target
01	JONES	LONDON	20000
02	SMITH	PARIS	25000
03	BROWN	EDINBURGH	15000
04	STEVENS	SWEDEN	40000
05	HARRIS	GLASGOW	10000
06	KING	NEW YORK	25000

CUSTOMERS

Customer Reference	Customer Name	Sales Area
01	Knight	LONDON
02	Klein	NEW YORK
03	Maurice	PARIS
04	Ericson	SWEDEN
05	Harris	EDINBURGH
06	Burt	LONDON
07	Ajax	GLASGOW
08	Worthing	LONDON
09	Tarn	EDINBURGH
10	Benson	NEW YORK

The column or attribute for the join will be Sales Area. It is the one on a
common domain. The result of the join will be a new table, RESULT:

RESULT

Salesman Number	Name	Sales Area	Target	Customer Reference	Customer Name	Sales Area
01	Jones	London	20000	01	Knight	London
01	Jones	London	20000	06	Burt	London
01	Jones	London	20000	08	Worthing	London
02	Smith	Paris	25000	03	Maurice	Paris
03	Brown	Edinburgh	15000	05	Harris	Edinburgh
03	Brown	Edinburgh	15000	09	Tarn	Edinburgh
04	Stevens	Sweden	40000	04	Ericson	Sweden
05	Harris	Glasgow	10000	07	Ajax	Glasgow
06	King	New York	25000	02	Klein	New York
06	King	New York	25000	10	Benson	New York

The first three records in RESULT are formed by joining the Salesman JONES record to those of each of his customers (references 01, 06 and 08) since these match on Sales Area 'LONDON'. The next record is formed by a match on 'PARIS', and so on.

It is worth noticing that if we projected the columns Salesman Number, Name, Sales Area and Target from the table RESULT we should arrive back at a table like SALESFORCE. There would be six records again, because the duplicates would be eliminated. Projection on other columns would produce a copy of CUSTOMERS.

Also, in practice, one of the two columns Sales Area would usually be eliminated from RESULT. In this way the column used for the join occurs once only in the RESULT.

The two tables that participate in the join can have different numbers of records (rows) and different numbers of attributes (columns). They would usually be joined on a similar pair of attributes, whose values would be drawn from a common domain or set of possible values. The join need not involve equality between values of the attributes. Other forms of join are implemented in, for example, INGRES (described in Chapter 10).

The join works as follows, at least conceptually:

— the first row of the first table is selected and the value is extracted from the column being used for the join;

— the other table is then examined on the matching column, taking records one by one until a match is found between the values in the two columns;

— when a match is found a new record is created for the new table. This record is formed by joining together the rows from the two tables;

— the process continues until the end of the second table is reached;

— the process is then repeated, taking the next row from the first table and scanning all the rows of the second table, until eventually the first table is exhausted.

The resulting new table might contain identical rows, but all but one of these are eliminated, since duplicates are not usually allowed in a relational table.

If we join the two tables below over P# the process described would produce four records for the two pairs shown. In each case these are two identical pairs, so only one of the pairs would usually be retained.

A	Name	P#		B	P#	Status
	X	P01			P01	S
	Y	P01			P01	T
	....	....			....	....

The two columns used for the join must contain comparable field values. The values of the two columns ought really to be taken from the same domain. For instance if one column contains values from the domain of possible dates, then the other column should also be on this same domain. It would make no sense if the second column was on the domain of sterling values, for instance.

It is evident that the method of operation just described would be very time-consuming if it were implemented in that way. Most modern systems contain powerful techniques that attempt to optimise the time taken to process queries. The join would seldom be implemented in the way just described.

There are several other relational operations which are discussed later.

TERMINOLOGY

The literature on relational systems uses unusual terminology, and the non-mathematical reader will find difficulty with some of the research work. Unfamiliar terms and notation obscure the meaning and value. The concepts are often quite familiar ones to data processing people. It is the words that are strange.

The following list shows some terms, with more familiar equivalents:

Relation: table or record type

Attribute: column name or field type

Element: field

Tuple: row or record occurrence (tuple rhymes with couple)

Degree: number of columns in a table

Cardinality: number of rows in a table

Precision of language is often essential. The definitions given are approximate equivalences.

An N-tuple is a record from a table with N columns. Binary relations are records with two columns. N-ary relations similarly are tables with N columns.

The term *relation* is sometimes used for a table, and sometimes for an instance of a record type.

The ideas of *attribute* and *domain* are distinct. All the values that occur in a specific field type, or column, are values of some attribute. These values are drawn from a *domain* of all possible values for that attribute. Many different field types can use the same domain (see Figure 1.1).

Terminology is still developing and many authors use their own variants in research papers, especially when developing further ideas.

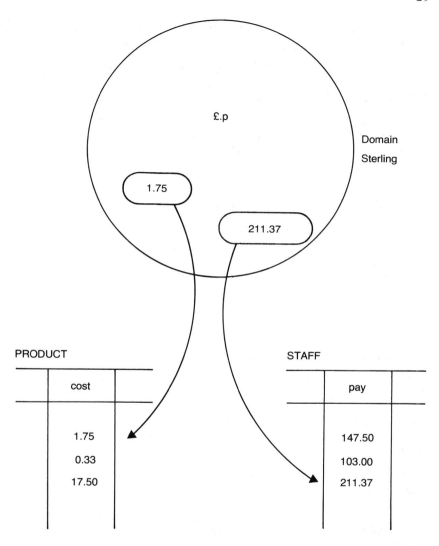

The attribute cost in table PRODUCT takes its values from the domain sterling.
The attribute pay in STAFF also draws its values from this same domain, sterling.

Figure 1.1   The Domain Concept

2 Relational Languages

GENERAL

Relational systems have been implemented in many different ways, using various languages. The rich variety of these languages sometimes obscures their underlying common basis.

The style of language has important consequences for any system. Some languages appeal particularly to one group, but are rejected by another. Personal taste and background have much influence.

LANGUAGE GROUPS

Three broad groups of languages can be identified, though particular systems may span more than one group.

Relational algebras include classical operations of mathematical set theory (union, intersection and difference) as well as the relational operators (select, project and join, outlined above). Often there are special operations for ordering a table, for summation and aggregation.

Relational calculus languages allow a new relation or table to be defined in terms of some operations on some existing tables. The calculus allows a result of a query to be defined in terms of relations in the database. An important language idea is the domain calculus, which will be examined below.

Query and display languages are intended to be easy to use and to exploit the facilities of display screens. Often they are hard to define, but great fun to use.

The relational language may be implemented as a system in various ways. The two very usual ways are to link it with a host language such as COBOL, PL/I or FORTRAN, or to incorporate it in some query or interrogation system.

Some languages are implemented in both situations, so that the same language can be used interactively and in mainstream database work.

In the next few sections we examine a number of different relational languages in the abstract, to see how the concepts might work. Several real implementations are described in later chapters. Much of the fundamental exploratory work was done on models rather than with real practical systems. What is described here is given for illustration rather than as a specification of any real system. This aids simplicity, and avoids 'freezing' a real system in a very quickly changing market.

Relational Algebras

A relational algebra is a collection of high-level operations on relations. We have described the three relational operations, *select, project* and *join*; the relational algebra includes also the traditional mathematical set operations, *union, intersection* and *difference*, together with a form of *Cartesian product*.

The two relations or tables for the set operations must be *union compatible*. That is to say they must be of the same degree, having the same number of attributes. Corresponding attributes in the two tables must be drawn from the same domain.

Union of two tables A and B, A UNION B, is the set of all tuples t belonging to either A or B or both. In other words, the Union of A and B produces a new table that contains all records from A and B, duplicates being eliminated.

Intersection of two tables A and B, A INTERSECT B, is the set of all tuples that occur in both tables. The result has all the records that occur in both table A and table B.

Difference between two tables A and B, A MINUS B, is the set of tuples belonging to A and not to B. The result contains the records that occur in A but not in B. The order is important, just as in arithmetic. A MINUS B is not the same as B MINUS A, just as $5 - 3$ is not the same as $3 - 5$.

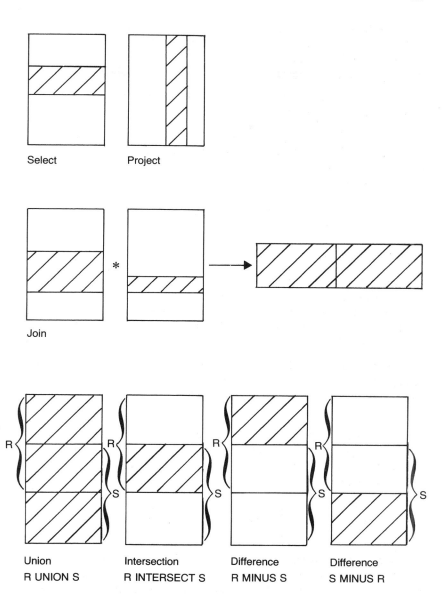

Figure 2.1 Relational Operations

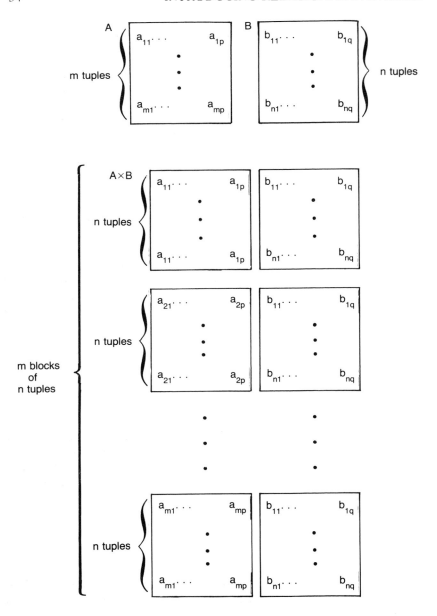

Figure 2.2   Cartesian Product A times B

The six operations (select, project, join, union, intersection and difference) are illustrated in Figure 2.1 The shaded portion shows the result of the operation. These diagrams are intended only as a guide. Notice that *select* and *project* are unary operations: they operate upon one table to produce another, shown as shaded. The result is a subset of the original table. For *join* the two tables can be as different as you like, but they must each have one attribute drawn from the same domain. The other three binary operations require that the two tables are set-compatible; in essence their columns must match; or, to put it another way, both tables must have the same sorts of records. (You cannot meaningfully start adding apples and step ladders!).

The other operation in the relational algebras is the extended *Cartesian product* (Figure 2.2). This is similar to the join operation. Given two relations A and B containing tuples a and b then A TIMES B is the set of all tuples t such that t is the concatenation of a tuple a and a tuple b. The concatenation of a tuple $a = (a_1 \ldots a_p)$ and a tuple $b = (b_1 \ldots b_q)$ is the tuple $t = (a_1 \ldots a_p \ b_1 \ldots b_q)$. Another way of looking at the extended Cartesian product is to think of it as the set of all possible records formed by taking a record from A and one from B and joining them together end to end.

If A is the set of all sizes of a product and B is the set of all colours from that product then A TIMES B is the set of all possible size/colour combinations.

The inverse operation *division* can also be defined, so that the system is complete. An example is given below, but in its simplest form we take as the dividend a binary relation A, that is to say one having two attributes, for example X and Y. The divisor B has one attribute Z. Suppose that attributes Y and Z are on the same domain, then we can divide A by B. DIVIDE A BY B OVER Y AND Z produces a quotient defined on the same domain as X.

The quotient X contains tuples X. The dividend A contains tuples (X, Y) and the divisor B contains tuples Y. A value X appears only if A contains pairs (X, Y) for *all* values of Y in B.

Consider an example. Suppose that A is a table of product size/colour pairs. We can divide using one or more colours as the divisor as shown in Table A.

TABLE A

SIZE	COLOUR
32	GREY
32	BLUE
32	WHITE
32	PINK
34	GREY
34	BLUE
34	WHITE
34	PINK
36	GREY
36	BLUE
36	PINK
38	GREY
38	PINK
40	GREY
40	PINK
42	GREY

Divisor

COLOUR
GREY

Divisor

COLOUR
WHITE

Divisor

COLOUR
BLUE
WHITE

Result

SIZE
32
34
36
38
40
42

Result

SIZE
32
34

Result

SIZE
32
34

One could also use SIZE as a divisor: getting colours as the result:

Divisor	SIZE
	38

Divisor	SIZE
	32
	38

Result	COLOUR
	GREY
	PINK

Result	COLOUR
	GREY
	PINK

One could project COLOUR from table A to get the set of all possible colours

Colours	COLOUR
	GREY
	BLUE
	WHITE
	PINK

Using this as divisor shows which sizes are available in all colours:

Result	SIZE
	32
	34

Similarly one could project SIZE to get a table of all sizes, and use that as divisor to get colours available in all sizes.

Sizes	SIZE
	32
	34
	36
	38
	40
	42

Result	COLOUR
	GREY

If size 42 had been available only in PINK and not in GREY the result would have been null.

Divide is very powerful, but hard to describe on higher order tables. It is in effect the inverse of the Cartesian product. Suppose that we consider the dividend table containing tuples (x, y) where x is a set of attributes and y is another set of attributes. Then we can divide this table by another table whose tuples z are another set of attributes. For this to be valid there must be one-to-one correspondence between the corresponding domains of the attributes in y and in z. The quotient will contain tuples that correspond in their domains to the x set of the original dividend.

The notation for relational algebras is straightforward. For instance the statement:

SELECT A WHERE SIZE = '38' GIVING MEDIUM

would produce a new table MEDIUM from table A showing the 38s:

SIZE	COLOUR
38	GREY
38	PINK

We could project this to give just the colours:

PROJECT MEDIUM OVER COLOUR GIVING MEDCOLS

One can combine the operations into one statement:

PROJECT (SELECT A WHERE SIZE = '38') OVER COLOUR GIVING MEDCOLS

Relational algebra operations can be nested one inside another using parentheses to show the bounds of the inner operations. The system will evaluate the inner operation and pass the result to the next outer layer, just as in ordinary algebra. Expressions can be nested one inside another, according to one's taste in these things. Sometimes it is clearer to set things out step by step. Nesting demonstrates the power of the technique, in that complex queries can be answered by a single statement.

Consider a slightly more advanced database with three tables; Line (for product line details), Supplier (for supplier details) and Supplier Line (to show which lines are supplied by each supplier).

Line

L

L#	SIZE	COLOUR
L01	32	GREY
L02	32	BLUE
L03	32	WHITE
L04	32	PINK
L05	34	GREY
L06	34	BLUE
L07	34	WHITE
L08	34	PINK
L09	36	GREY
L10	36	BLUE
L11	36	PINK
L12	38	GREY
L13	38	PINK
L14	40	GREY
L15	40	PINK
L16	42	GREY

Supplier

S

S#	STATUS	CITY
S01	10	LONDON
S02	20	PARIS
S03	15	BRUSSELS
S04	40	NEW YORK

Supplier Line

SL	S#	L#
	S01	L01
	S01	L02
	S01	L03
	S01	L04
	S01	L05
	S02	L15
	S03	L16
	S04	L02
	etc	etc

To select suppliers in LONDON we can write

SELECT S WHERE CITY = 'LONDON'

To select suppliers of BLUE lines we can write

SELECT L WHERE COLOUR = 'BLUE' GIVING TEMP1

JOIN TEMP1 AND SL OVER L# GIVING TEMP2

PROJECT TEMP2 OVER S# GIVING RESULT

TEMP1 is a table containing all the records from L that are 'BLUE' so to speak. The join uses this result with SL to give TEMP2. Notice that the records will only be joined where a match occurs on L#. Finally we project column S# to pick out the suppliers and eliminate the duplicates to give a compact list. This query can be nested, like this:

PROJECT (JOIN(SELECT L WHERE COLOUR = 'BLUE')

AND SL OVER L#)

OVER S#

GIVING RESULT

We can select the supplier city for suppliers who provide line L02:

SELECT FROM SL WHERE L# = L02 GIVING TEMP1

PROJECT TEMP1 OVER S# GIVING TEMP2

JOIN TEMP2 AND S OVER S# GIVING TEMP3

PROJECT TEMP3 OVER CITY GIVING RESULT

The first project is not strictly necessary, but it makes the join more manageable. We could write the same query in nested form:

PROJECT (JOIN (SELECT FROM SL WHERE L# = L02)

AND S OVER S#)

OVER CITY

GIVING RESULT

The conditions for the selection can be compound, and one can link across the database using join. For instance one could find the city of origin for PINK lines by the following:

SELECT FROM L WHERE COLOUR = 'PINK' GIVING T1

JOIN T1 AND SL OVER L# GIVING T2

PROJECT T2 OVER S# GIVING T3

JOIN T3 AND S OVER S# GIVING T4

PROJECT T4 OVER CITY GIVING RESULT

or, nested:

PROJECT (JOIN(JOIN(SELECT FROM L WHERE COLOUR
= 'PINK'

AND SL OVER L#)

AND S OVER S#)

OVER CITY

GIVING RESULT

Suppose we want the status and city for those suppliers who supply all the lines:

PROJECT L OVER L# GIVING T1

DIVIDE SL BY T1 OVER L# GIVING T2

JOIN T2 AND S OVER S# GIVING T3

PROJECT T3 OVER STATUS, CITY GIVING RESULT

or nested:

PROJECT(JOIN(DIVIDE SL BY(PROJECT L OVER L#)

OVER L#)

AND S OVER S#)

OVER STATUS, CITY

GIVING RESULT

To insert and delete items from tables we can use UNION and MINUS. To add a new line to table L, say size 44 colour PINK, we could write:

L UNION $\Big(($'L17', '44', 'PINK'$)\Big)$ GIVING L

One could remove supplier S04 using MINUS by writing:

S MINUS $\Big(($'S04', '40', 'NEW YORK'$)\Big)$ GIVING S

In practice one might use a wild value such as ? for most of the items, so that one could for instance delete all size 34s from table L by writing:

L MINUS $\Big(($?, '34',?$)\Big)$ GIVING L

which would save writing out all the tuples separately, or even needing to know what they were.

The relational algebra is very powerful. It provides a compact, yet precise, notation. It is relationally complete, in the sense that it contains all the algebraic operations.

The language is fairly non-procedural, in that you specify the result that is wanted, rather than how to compute it. The nested forms allow the database management system to optimise the processing, retaining only what is needed to achieve the end result. Of course the implementors of a system would need to devise powerful techniques to optimise in this way. Some success has been achieved here. Optimisation is commonplace in ordinary high-level language implementations. There is hope therefore that the very cheap computing power that is now available could be used to secure economies in this area.

SQL

The most widely used language is probably SQL which is discussed in Chapter 8. In SQL the basic query construct is the SELECT-FROM-WHERE command. It forms the basis for retrieval.

Suppose that we wanted to know the name of employee number 43 from the table EMPLOYEES. The appropriate command would be:

SELECT   ENAME

FROM   EMPLOYEES

WHERE   ENO = 43;

The SELECT clause specifies the names of the fields (columns or attributes) that are to be selected – in this case one, but there can be several. The FROM clause names the table to be used. The selection conditions are given in the WHERE clause.

One can specify just which columns are wanted. If all the details are needed an asterisk can be used:

SELECT *

FROM EMPLOYEES

WHERE ENO = 43;

would give the whole of the record for employee 43.

Compound selections can be specified in the WHERE clause. More than one table can be used in the selection. The first way of doing this is to embed or nest a SELECT-FROM-WHERE command inside the WHERE clause, so that some column value(s) are matched to values selected from another table:

SELECT columns chosen from table A

FROM records in table A

WHERE table A column = (SELECT table B column

FROM records in table B

WHERE condition)

In effect, the query examines or extracts from table B a set of records that match the 'condition' specified in the nested WHERE clause. The value in some attribute column of table B in these selected table B records is then matched with a corresponding attribute in table A ("WHERE table A column = "). Records from table A are selected where the match occurs. The SELECTed result is "columns chosen from table A", from these records.

The attribute chosen for matching needs to be on the same domain in the two tables. It might be employee number for instance, or date.

Notice that there are four columns or sets of columns involved in the query:

SELECT *col1*

FROM table A

WHERE *col2* = (SELECT *col3*

FROM table B

WHERE condition on *col4*)

One or more columns denoted by *col1* could be selected from table A. *Col2* in table A could be included in *col1* set or not. Often it would be wanted for display, anyway. The *col2* of table A and *col3* of table B must match from the same domains. The *col4* of table B could be one or more columns depending upon the complexity of the query. *Col3* could be included in the conditions or not.

The second way of using two tables in a query is the joining methods. The WHERE clause links the two tables by specifying the columns that were to be matched.

SELECT Columns (from table A & table B)

FROM Table A, table B

WHERE Column from A = column from B

This is an implicit join operation, followed by a select.

SQL has a whole range of data manipulation and data definition commands which are discussed in Chapter 8.

Relational Calculus

Queries in the relational calculus languages are of the form:

<target>WHERE <predicate>

in which <target> specifies the tables (relations) and attributes required, and <predicate> gives the properties or conditions that must be satisfied.

The relational calculus is simply a notation for expressing the definition of some new table or relation in terms of some existing tables. It is a notation for expressing the result of a query in terms of relations we have already.

Let us examine an example of relational calculus notation. One might ask for the names and reference numbers of customers in Paris by the expression:

$$\{(Customer.Name, Customer.Reference): Customer.City = 'Paris'\}$$

The braces $\{$ and $\}$ indicate that this is a set definition. We are defining a new table. The two attributes of the new table are Customer.Name and Customer.Reference, listed in parentheses. The colon stands for 'where'. The predicate – the property or condition required – is that Customer.City should be 'Paris'.

In practice abbreviations are often used and the above expression might appear as:

$$\{(C.Name, C.Ref): C.City='Paris'\}$$

or even as:

$$\{(C.N,C.R.): C.C='Paris'\}$$

The relational calculus languages employ the concept of a variable, which acts as a place-holder in the table or relation. A tuple-variable ranges over a table. In effect it represents a record (or tuple) in the relation. In the customer table we could select names of customers in Paris by the expression.

$$\{(Customer.Name): Customer.City = 'Paris'\}$$

We can represent the customer table by a variable X which ranges over Customer:

Range of X is Customer

$$\{(X.Name): X.City = 'Paris'\}$$

X is a range variable. It refers to some tuple or record in Customer.

Obviously this can save a good deal of writing, especially if the table names are long.

A more important reason is that in the calculus languages a single query may require the use of a single table or relation in two or more distinct ways. These distinct uses must be distinguished in the notation. In effect we need to use two or more tuples from one table simultaneously to answer the query.

For instance "Get the employee number of every employee who earns more than his manager" could be addressed to a table showing "employee number, employee's manager, salary". Clearly we need to extract from the table the employee, and then (from the same table) extract the details for the employee's manager, so as to find the manager's salary.

We therefore employ a variable to represent one of these uses of the table. This is a range variable or tuple variable, which ranges over a relation, representing some tuple in the relation.

We might define the employee relation or table as:

STAFF(EMP# : E# , ENAME : NAME , MGR : E# ...)

representing a table like this:

STAFF

EMP#	ENAME	MGR . .
E01	JONES	E02
E02	SMITH	E19
E03	BROWN	E04
E04	ELLIS	E19
etc		

We could define: Range of X is STAFF. This means that X is a variable that ranges over STAFF. The expression X(EMP#) or X.EMP# refers to the employee serial number of some record or tuple in the STAFF table. Similarly we can use X(ENAME) or X.ENAME to refer to the name attribute of some record in the STAFF table. (The notation is by no means fixed.)

For the query just given "Get the employee number of every employee who earns more than his manager" we need another element in the table, to hold employee salary. Our relation or table is thus:

STAFF(EMP*#* : E*#* , ENAME : NAME , MGR : E*#* , SAL : SALARY)

We can use two variables X and XM for the records of the desired employees and their managers respectively.

We write:

X   range STAFF

XM range STAFF

The set we require is:

$\Big\{$(X.EMP*#*) where $\exists$ (XM.EMP*#* = X.MGR and

XM.SAL<X.SAL)$\Big\}$

The symbol $\exists$ is read "there exists". One can imagine XM as holding one tuple from the table and X as holding another. We find all the X tuples that exist that satisfy the condition, using XM to examine the corresponding manager's tuple.

In fact of course we need only one tuple variable in this case:

X range STAFF

$\Big\{$(X.EMP*#*)   where $\exists$ (STAFF.EMP*#* = X.MGR and

STAFF.SAL<X.SAL)$\Big\}$

does the same job.

Another approach is to use *domain variables*. A domain variable ranges over one of the database domains. Such a variable is a place holder for a value from a database domain:

Range of X is E*#*

means that X is a domain variable whose values are employee serial numbers. This contrasts with range or tuple variables whose value is one record or tuple from the table. We could have a variable Y on the domain of dates by writing Range of Y is DATE.

A relational calculus using domain variables is called a domain relational calculus. One using tuple variables is called a tuple relational calculus.

Relational algebra, tuple relational calculus and domain relational calculus mark three positions in the spectrum of query languages.

Another approach is provided by the display-oriented languages. Ease of use is one of the primary design aims, rather than mathematical elegance.

Query by Example

Query by Example (developed at the IBM Yorktown Heights Research Laboratory) is designed for use with visual display terminals. It is an example of a display oriented language system. The system was devised as a query system originally, but has been extended.

One or more tables are used in the query which procedes as a dialogue between the user and the system. A table is built-up at the terminal. The user supplies some parts – to direct the search and define what is wanted. The system supplies other parts.

In a simple query the user types in the name of a table that can answer the query. It might be the size/colour table that we called A. The system would respond with the table headings (the attribute names) like this:

A	SIZE	COLOUR

To find what sizes are available in a particular colour one types P. for 'Print' followed by a sample size number underlined in the SIZE column and the required colour under the COLOUR column:

A	SIZE	COLOUR
	P. 44	PINK

The 44, underlined, is an example element, to show what kind of result is wanted. PINK is a content element. It is not underlined, and indicates that the result must be PINK. The query could be specified as 'Print all sizes available in PINK". Notice that <u>44</u> is simply an example of the kind of thing that is wanted. The entry <u>44</u> does not need to occur in the attributes of the table entry. It is merely an example. We could have used anything else like <u>CAT</u> or <u>3.</u> It is a domain variable, in fact.

The example elements are used to establish connections between rows in more complex queries. Here we could have omitted the example and simply typed P. thus:

A	SIZE	COLOUR
	P.	PINK

One could obtain all sizes by the query:

A	SIZE	COLOUR
	P.<u>SZ</u>	

or all colours by:

A	SIZE	COLOUR
		P.<u>COL</u>

or all available size/colour combinations by:

A	SIZE	COLOUR
	P.<u>SZ</u>	P.<u>COL</u>

But this can be simplified to:

A	SIZE	COLOUR
P.		

that is, print the table, which is convenient if the table has six or seven attributes.

One can qualify the retrieval. Get colours for sizes above 36, for example:

A	SIZE	COLOUR
	>36	P.PINK

Remember that PINK is here simply as an example. It does not matter whether PINK exists as an attribute in the table. Any of the comparison operators $=, \neq, <, \leq, >, \geq$, can be used in this way. It is normal to omit $=$ and simply write the attribute. For instance to get the colours for size 38 we would write:

A	SIZE	COLOUR
	38	P.RED

We can qualify the retrieval in other ways. To get sizes available in PINK and BLUE we need to use two lines:

A	SIZE	COLOUR
	P.99	PINK
	99	BLUE

This will AND together the two conditions before producing the result. Notice that we are not doing two queries here, just one. To get sizes for PINK and also sizes for BLUE we need two queries:

A	SIZE	COLOUR
	P.99	PINK

A	SIZE	COLOUR
	P.99	BLUE

In the PINK and BLUE example the 99 acts as a *link* between the two rows. Links are very important in Query By Example, because they allow one to reference elements from different tables in the same query.

Consider the Line-Supplier database, which we used earlier, shown on page 52. The Line table, L, shows each of the 16 lines of stock, with the Line number L#, the Size and the Colour. The Supplier table, S, shows four suppliers with three attributes, Supplier number S#, Status and City. The third table, Supplier Line table, SL, shows which suppliers provide which lines with the attributes Supplier number S# and Line number L#.

We can perform more interesting queries on this database. For instance we can ask for suppliers located in LONDON with status >20 by the query:

S	S#	STATUS	CITY
	P.S99	>20	LONDON

and find that there are none. So we could ask about suppliers either with status >20 or located in LONDON:

S	S#	STATUS	CITY
	P.S99	>20	
	S99		LONDON

Here the S99 acts as a link between the two parts of the query. To obtain the OR condition two rows are needed. Two conditions in the same row are taken to be ANDed together. The query is in effect asking for the union of suppliers with status >20 with those located in LONDON. An inclusive OR is implied.

We can obtain supplier City for suppliers who supply line L02 ('size 32 blue') by the query:

S	S#	STATUS	CITY		SL	S#	L#
	SX		P.CITY			SX	L02

Line

L

L#	SIZE	COLOUR
L01	32	GREY
L02	32	BLUE
L03	32	WHITE
L04	32	PINK
L05	34	GREY
L06	34	BLUE
L07	34	WHITE
L08	34	PINK
L09	36	GREY
L10	36	BLUE
L11	36	PINK
L12	38	GREY
L13	38	PINK
L14	40	GREY
L15	40	PINK
L16	42	GREY

Supplier

S

S#	STATUS	CITY
S01	10	LONDON
S02	20	PARIS
S03	15	BRUSSELS
S04	40	NEW YORK

Supplier Line

SL

S#	L#
S01	L01
S01	L02
S01	L03
S01	L04
S01	L05
S02	L15
S03	L16
S04	L02
etc	etc

Here two tables S and SL are employed. P.CITY means print City name. The SX in each of the tables acts as a link between them. L02 (not underlined) specifies which line number is wanted. We should expect the result to include LONDON (since supplier S01 supplies line L02) and NEW YORK (supplier S04 also supplies L02).

We can link more than two tables in Query By Example. For instance, get suppliers of BLUE lines:

S	S#	STATUS	CITY
P.	SX		

SL	S#	L#
	SX	LX

L	L#	SIZE	COLOUR
	LX		BLUE

Here we ask for printing of supplier details (P.) using SX to link between the S and SL tables and LX to link between the SL and L tables.

A negation operator is available in Query By Example. (It is often easier to specify what you don't want, rather than what you do.) The NOT operator is ⌐. For example, get line numbers of lines that are not BLUE:

L	L#	SIZE	COLOUR
⌐	P.LX		BLUE

One can print a result containing details drawn from more than one table. For instance, print for each line all supplier details:

L	L#	SIZE	COLOUR
	LX		

SL	S#	L#
	SX	LX

S	S#	STATUS	CITY
	SX	ST	SC

RESULT	L#	S#	STATUS	CITY
	P.LX	P.SX	P.ST	P.SC

Here the user creates a new table of the same shape as the result. It can be given any name and attribute names that one wants. The names can be left blank. LX acts as a link for the line number and similarly for the other details.

Another operation is ALL which can be used to qualify an example. For instance ALL.LX in table L would refer to all line numbers:

L	L#	SIZE	COLOUR
	ALL.LX		

We could print a list of suppliers who supply all lines by the query:

SL	S#	L#
	P.SX	ALL.LX

Query By Example has many other interesting features. The relational operators tend to be hidden from the user. Many of the examples given imply *select, project* and *join* operations, which are of course fundamental to the relational approach.

One must not overlook the implications for processing capacity. It is very easy in the relational languages to specify a very complex enquiry, perhaps on several large tables. If the query is entered through a VDU instantaneous response may be expected. Disappointment may be evident if it is not forthcoming! Suppose that the database just considered had several hundreds or thousands of suppliers for a multitude of product lines. The queries would take no longer to formulate, but the results might be delayed, at least a little while.

Most relational languages include built-in functions as well as the relational and logical operations. Examples are COUNT, AVERAGE, MAX, MIN and SUM.

3 Keys and Normalisation

KEYS

Reference numbers are often used to identify things: invoice numbers, part codes, serial numbers are common examples. Often combinations of letters and digits are used, as in car index registration marks. In data processing, keys are used for similar purposes. Keys serve to identify records so that they can be referenced or accessed. Records in a file are often sequenced by key value. Key and key value are fundamental ideas in data processing. Clearly therefore the relational approach must incorporate facilities for handling keys. In fact relational systems have special rules about keys.

A key must be formed from one or more attributes in the records or relations. A *candidate key* is a combination of attributes in any tuple (record) in the table that uniquely distinguishes that tuple (record) from any other in the table. In other words the candidate key must be unique. It is always possible to form such a unique key in a relational system, because there are no duplicate records. A further rule is that if any attribute is dropped from the candidate key then the uniqueness property is lost. This means that any candidate key must have sufficient attributes to identify each record uniquely, but should not contain redundant attributes.

It is often possible to consider several candidate keys, ie different combinations of attributes that would give uniqueness for the key.

Consider for example the simple table, PRODUCT, below, in which size and colour are related.

PRODUCT

P#	SIZE	COLOUR
P01	8	RED
P02	10	GREEN
P03	12	BLUE
P04	14	YELLOW

The product is one that is colour-coded by size. Any one of the three attributes would be a candidate key. A key formed from two attributes would give over-kill. In the combination P# with SIZE for example either could be dropped without loss of uniqueness.

Suppose that the product is made in two lengths, still colour coded by size, probably the diameter.

LPRODUCT

P#	SIZE	COLOUR	LENGTH
P01	8	RED	50
P02	10	GREEN	50
P03	12	BLUE	50
P04	14	YELLOW	50
P05	8	RED	100
P06	10	GREEN	100
P07	12	BLUE	100
P08	14	YELLOW	100

Now we can still use P# as a candidate key, but SIZE and COLOUR are no longer sufficient on their own, or together. The other two candidate keys are SIZE-LENGTH or COLOUR-LENGTH. This table has four attributes and three candidate keys.

Consider the table LINE (discussed earlier).

LINE

L#	SIZE	COLOUR
L01	32	GREY
L02	32	BLUE
L03	32	WHITE
L04	32	PINK
L05	34	GREY
L06	34	BLUE
L07	34	WHITE
L08	34	PINK
L09	36	GREY
L10	36	BLUE
L11	36	PINK
L12	38	GREY
L13	38	PINK
L14	40	GREY
L15	40	PINK
L16	42	GREY

Here the sizes are not colour coded! There are, by inspection, two candidate keys L# and SIZE-COLOUR. This would hold good unless we introduce two product lines with the same SIZE-COLOUR, eg

L#	SIZE	COLOUR
L17	44	GREY
L18	44	GREY

after which only L# would be a suitable candidate key. (One assumes lines 17 and 18 differ in some way that is not specified, like style, otherwise they would normally be given the same line number, L#.) Other combinations of attributes such as L#–SIZE and L#–COLOUR are not candidate keys, because one of the pair can be eliminated without loss of uniqueness.

A *primary key* is a candidate key in which no component can be set to null. Primary keys are intended to provide a simple and clear representation of real-world objects. Attempts to change the value of a primary key must be carefully controlled. This is because the primary key may occur again in other parts of the database. The primary key acts as a cross-reference. Any change to a primary key will usually mean that other occurrences of the key will need to be changed.

Consider the record L16 in table LINE just given:

LINE

L#	SIZE	COLOUR
.	.	.
L15	40	PINK
L16	42	GREY

It is the only size 42 in the range. Knowing this fact the COLOUR attribute might have been omitted. In the real world we might have regarded the colour of size 42s as unimportant, or even not known. The COLOUR would have been null, thus:

L#	SIZE	COLOUR
L16	42	–

This means that there are still two candidate keys in the table LINE (L01 – L16) viz L# and SIZE-COLOUR; both candidate keys are unique.

Now that colour can be null, however, only one of these two keys is a primary key. L# is a primary key, but SIZE-COLOUR is not.

Why are primary keys so important? Every item in a relational database can be uniquely addressed by the three-part combination:

  relational (table) name   R

  primary key value   K

  attribute (column) name   A

This is unique over the database. It is associative and not positional. Access to the item does not depend upon other items in the database.

What if there are no primary keys? There are problems, which were hinted at by L17 and L18 (44-GREYs) above. Consider a customer table C.

C

C#	NAME	T#
C01	BROWN	–
–	BROWN	T05
–	SMITH	T05

We have null values appearing in customer number C# and territory number T#. Possible candidate keys are C#– NAME and NAME–T#. No individual attribute is a candidate key, because all contain more than one record with the same value or nulls.

There is however no satisfactory primary key. The uncertainty concerns the name BROWN. Is there one BROWN or two? We cannot tell. This kind of uncertainty is very common when things or events are recorded without a unique serial number or mark. Manufactured batches or shipments might be identified by date and description:

SUPPLY

S#	L#	DATE	QTY
S5	–	17.7.82	57
–	L19	17.7.82	57

We might guess that this represents one shipment. What about this, though?

SUPPLY

S#	L#	DATE	QTY
S174	L19	10.11.82	2000
S175	–	10.11.82	2000
–	L19	10.11.82	2000

It might be that 2000 is a standard quantity. Did we have two shipments on the same day, or three? To eliminate this problem the primary key must not contain null values.

Update of primary keys needs careful control. This is to be expected, since such keys are very important for access to data items. Primary keys from some tables are often used in other tables. The line number L# identifying the product supplied is an example:

LINE

L#	SIZE	COLOUR
L01	32	GREY
L02	32	BLUE
⋮	⋮	⋮
L16	42	GREY
L17	32	YELLOW
L18	32	BROWN

SUPPLY

S#	L#	DATE	QTY
..	..	..	..
S1743	L02	10.1.83	100
S1744	L01	10.1.83	200

The primary key L# of LINE is used in SUPPLY to reference the kind of goods supplied. Any change to the primary key of table LINE would clearly have implications for the table SUPPLY.

Some bright spark might decide to rationalise the product line numbers. If this was done on table LINE alone, then the table SUPPLY would become meaningless. The key L02 might disappear, or worse still, it might denote SIZE 38, BROWN in the new scheme.

The primary key of a tuple is often used as a reference to it elsewhere in the database. The integrity of the key as a reference is vital. Special techniques have to be devised to preserve the *referential integrity* of these keys. Ordinary update cannot be allowed, without danger of compromising this kind of integrity. It is discussed in Chapter 6.

The interim solution is to authorise only a few experts to update primary keys. It is assumed that these experts will appreciate the problems and take care.

The second solution is to force deletion and re-insertion of all affected records. Ordinary update of primary keys is not allowed. This does not solve the problem, but it prevents duplicate keys appearing in affected tables.

NORMALISATION

Any data structure can be modelled in various ways. The relational model is one such way. Any data model should be efficient. It should provide reasonable access to the data, particularly for the most frequent requirements. It should allow restructuring without difficulty, when requirements change. A new data item might be needed, for example. We do not want the design of the logical data structure to restrict flexibility in the use of the data, or subsequent changes.

Normalisation is a technique that has been developed to ensure that the data structure is efficient. It stems from the work of E F Codd, and was invented for use in relational systems. It has far wider applications, however. Normalisation is the formal expression of the way many good designers work. It provides a means of describing the logical structure of the data in an information system. The benefits of normalisation are:

— freedom from undesirable insertion, update and deletion dependencies. In the next section an example is used to show these dependencies and how normalisation removes them;

— restructuring of the data is minimised when new data is introduced. Data independence is improved by allowing extensions to
be made to a database with little or no effect on existing application programs that access the database;

— no artificial constraints are placed on the data structures.

The basic principles of normalisation are widely used as a tool in the
design of information systems. Though the technique was devised for use
in relational systems it must be stressed that normalisation can be used as
a tool in the design of any information system. It can be used with
conventional files as well as with database management systems.

Normalisation involves three stages which are carried out in order.
Performance of the second stage always implies that the first stage is
completed, and similarly for later stages. After each stage has been
completed the data is said to be in first, second or third normal form.
These are abbreviated to 1NF, 2NF, 3NF or to FNF, SNF or TNF. (The
original work on normalisation by E F Codd proposed the three stages. A
Fourth Normal Form has been defined but has not won general accep-
tance, and is not considered further.)

First normal form relations are a subset of the universe of all possible

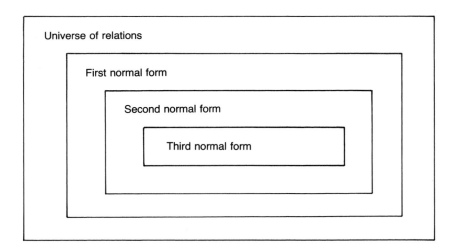

Figure 3.1   Normal Form Relations

relations. Similarly second normal form relations are a subset of first normal forms. Third normal form relations are a subset of second normal forms. This is illustrated in Figure 3.1.

Codd's normalisation process consists of three rules or steps which transform unnormalised relations into third normal form. It is this TNF which we need for the relational system.

First Normal Form

The essence of first normal form (FNF) is that:

A record in first normal form does not include any repeating groups.

The formal definition is: 'A relation is in first normal form if it has the property that none of its domains has elements which are themselves sets.'

A relation which is not in first normal form is called an unnormalised relation. A normalised relation can be represented in a flat file in which each n-tuple is a record in fixed format.

An example will be used to demonstrate the normalisation process and discuss the advantages that it provides. Consider a system in which an order for a number of products is sent to a supplier. Such an order may have the format shown in Figure 3.2.

Analysis of this order shows that the data listed below is of interest. Order numbers are unique, and are generally used to reference a particular order so the 'order number' is assumed to be a key. An underlined data-item is a key.

<u>Order Number</u>

Date

Supplier Number

Supplier Name

Supplier Address

Product Number

Product Description

Product Price

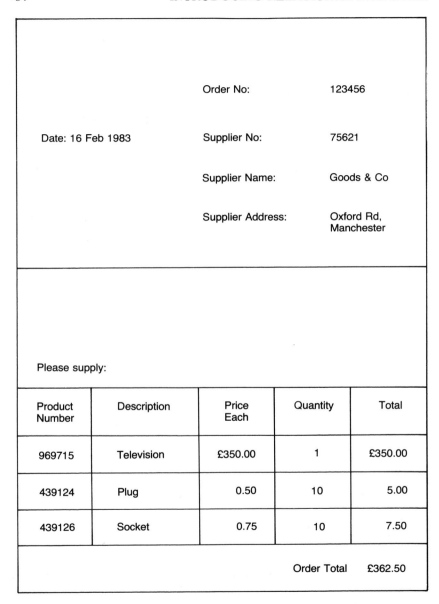

Figure 3.2   Possible Order Format

Product Quantity

Product Total Price

Order Total Price

In relational form this would be written

ORDER FORM (<u>Order Number</u>, Order Date, Supplier Number, Supplier Name, Supplier Address, Product Number, Product Description, Product Price, Product Quantity, Product Total Price, Order Total Price).

This order form contains a repeating group, because the order can contain more than one order line – several products can be ordered on one order. Removal of this repeating group produces the following FNF relations (where the keys are underlined):

<u>Order Number</u>

Date

Supplier Number

Supplier Name

Supplier Address

Order Total Price

<u>Order Number</u>

<u>Product Number</u>

Product Description

Product Price

Product Quantity

Product Total Price

Notice that both FNF relations carry the key (Order Number) of the unnormalised relation. In order to enable individual products on a given order to be identified, the second relation has a compound key comprising Order Number and Product Number.

The removal of repeating groups make the relations easier to understand because the data can be represented as a number of simple tables. From the physical point of view FNF relations can be implemented as flat files, ie files with fixed length records.

The unnormalised form would have to be implemented as a multi-record type file or contain records of variable length. Both methods increase the complexity of the storage mechanism, and of the programs that access the data. Variable length records usually have an upper limit on length, so problems are encountered with long order forms. FNF removes these problems. One can have any number of records in the second relation, so that order forms of any length can be accommodated.

There are problems with FNF. Information about a product can be recorded only if, for example, there is an order for it in the system. (The second relation has a key that uses <u>Order Number</u> with <u>Product Number</u>.) There are problems with the three basic storage operations; insertion, deletion and update:

— information about a product cannot be inserted unless there is an order for that product;

— if an order line-item is deleted, then information about the product is lost;

— every order line-item for a given product replicates the product information. If any detail, such as price, changes, the many occurrences will need to be changed or updated.

There are similar problems with supplier details.

Second Normal Form

Within any second normal form (SNF) record, each field (or attribute or data item) depends on the whole key and not on only part of the key.

The formal definition is: 'A relation R is in second normal form if it is in first normal form and every non-prime atttribute of R is fully functionally dependent on each candidate key of R.'

A non-prime attribute is an attribute that is not part of the key. This definition is saying that every data-item (attribute) must be dependent on the whole key of the relation, not just part of a compound key. Partial key dependencies must be removed. The step applies only to relations with compound keys. In fact FNF relations without compound keys are in SNF already.

In the example, the dependencies of the following relation need to be examined since it has a compound key.

<u>Order Number</u>

<u>Product Number</u>

Product Description

Product Price

Product Quantity

Product Total Price

Clearly, 'Product Quantity' and 'Product Total Price' are dependent on both 'Order Number' and 'Product Number'. The whole key is needed to uniquely identify these two data-items. On the other hand, 'Product Description' and 'Product Price' are both dependent on 'Product Number', but not on 'Order Number'. These dependencies can be illustrated diagrammatically as shown below.

<u>Order Number</u>

<u>Product Number</u>

Product Description

Product Price

Product Quantity

Product Total Price

The SNF relations for the example are thus:

<u>Order Number</u> (unchanged from FNF)

Date

Supplier Number

Supplier Name

Supplier Address

Order Total Price

Product Number

Product Description

Product Price

Order Number

Product Number

Product Quantity

Product Total Price

The problems with the FNF are resolved in SNF. The product information is held on a separate relation. Product information can be inserted, deleted and amended without the need for an order. Care would still be needed in handling the situation where information about products with outstanding orders is to be updated or deleted.

There are still problems with this SNF representation. The relation with the key Order Number poses similar problems to those we discussed about product information. Supplier information is the difficulty in the example, and we have problems with insertion, deletion and update, just as we did with product information.

We cannot insert supplier information unless there is an order. We lose supplier information when orders are deleted. Every order replicates supplier information. If the information changes, as when a supplier changes his address, then all occurrences would need to be updated.

Third Normal Form

As one might anticipate, this is an extension of second normal form. Second normal form eliminates dependencies on a partial key. Third normal form (TNF) removes dependencies on any other non-key fields.

Within any third normal form relation, each field depends only on the key, and does not depend on any other fields within the relation. A third normal form record is also in second normal form.

The formal definition is: 'A relation R is in third normal form if it is second normal form and every non-prime attribute of R is non-transitively dependent on each candidate key of R.'

A non-prime attribute is one that is not part of the key.

If A ──▶ B and B ──▶ C implies A ──▶ C, then C is said to be transitively dependent on A. In other words if C is dependent on B and B is dependent on A implies that C is dependent on A, then we say that C is transitively dependent on A.

The definition says that there should be no transitive dependencies between data items which are not part of the key (ie non-prime attributes). SNF is concerned with data item dependencies on the key. In contrast TNF is concerned with dependencies between non-key data items in the relation.

Examination of the SNF example above does not reveal any transitive dependencies in the second and third relations with the keys <u>Product Number</u> and <u>Order Number/Product Number</u>. The first relation with Key Order Number is more interesting.

<u>Order Number</u>

Date

Supplier Number

Supplier Name

Supplier Address

Order Total Price

Each non-key data-item is considered in turn to see whether it has any dependencies on any other non-key data-item in the relation. 'Date' and 'Order Total Price' are not dependent on any of the Supplier data-items. However, 'Supplier Number' implies 'Supplier Name' and 'Supplier Address'. So there are transitive dependencies in this relation. This can be shown as:

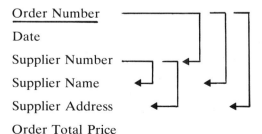

The TNF relations for the example are thus:

<u>Order Number</u>

Date

Supplier Number

Order Total Price

<u>Supplier Number</u>

Supplier Name

Supplier Address

<u>Product Number</u>

Product Description

Product Price

<u>Order Number</u>

<u>Product Number</u>

Product Quantity

Product Total Price

A separate relation now contains the supplier information. Supplier information may thus be inserted, deleted and updated even if an order does not exist. Naturally, care would need to be taken when deleting or updating supplier information if orders are outstanding against them.

In relational notation we could express this as follows:

ORDER (<u>Order Number,</u> Date, Supplier Number, Order Total Price)

SUPPLIER (<u>Supplier Number</u>, Supplier Name, Supplier Address)

PRODUCT (<u>Product Number,</u> Product Description, Product Price)

LINE ITEM (<u>Order Number</u>, <u>Product Number,</u> Product Quantity, Product Total Price)

The relations in TNF have eliminated the problems associated with supplier information in SNF.

PRACTICAL NORMALISATION

Normalisation is a very practical way of organising and establishing data structure and a data model. It can be applied outside the database environment, even though it was developed for use in relational systems.

Normalisation is a basis for many of the formal system design techniques now being marketed by consultancies, software houses and manufacturers.

A typical practical approach uses normalisation in data analysis. The first step is to find natural relationships between data-items irrespective of future design considerations. In other words, one wants to discover the pure natural relationships. These can be expressed as unnormalised relations, just as we did with the order example earlier in this chapter.

The unnormalised relations are converted into first normal form (FNF) by creating

1 a relation from the fields that are unique

2 a relation from the fields that repeat.

If the relation contains a compound key it must be transformed into second normal form.

This is done by creating a separate relation comprising those data items which are wholly dependent on the compound key. The process is repeated for data items that are dependent on part of the compound key.

We now have a set of relations in second normal form, SNF. We examine each relation to determine whether the non-key items are dependent on each other. If any are found we create a separate relation for them, to transform the SNF relations into TNF.

At this stage the TNF can be optimised. There may be some degenerate relations consisting only of a key. These can usually be eliminated. Other relations may have the same key, and can be combined to form one relation, provided the result makes sense and is meaningful. If anomalies are discovered in this optimisation process it is usually because there is some ambiguity in the underlying data.

Experienced analysts and designers will often produce TNF relations as a matter of course, without realising that they are doing so. They use common sense and experience and write down normalised relations. The formal normalisation technique provides a means for verifying the soundness of such solutions.

The data model produced by the normalisation process provides a means for assessing proposed changes to meet new demands or changed circumstances. The modifications can be added to the model which can be checked to see that it is still in TNF. The modifications may involve additions to existing relations, or the addition of new relations to the model, and probably both.

Normalisation is a useful technique in any circumstances. It is almost essential if you are to make full use of the relational approach.

4 Logical Structuring and Data Independence

INTRODUCTION

A database is a collection of stored data organised in such a way that all user requirements are satisfied by the database. In general there is only one copy of each item of data although there may be some controlled repetition of some data. A relational database is one of the kinds of database organisation. Others are the network and the hierarchical approaches.

A database management system – a DBMS – is a general-purpose set of programs that aid and control each user's access to and use of the database for adding, modifying and retrieving data and this includes facilities for giving data independence, integrity and security.

A database management system must provide appropriate facilities to support these aims. In this chapter we examine two aspects of support: data independence and structuring facilities.

Access control is discussed in the next chapter. Questions of integrity, recovery and restart are discussed in Chapter 6. Language facilities have been discussed already.

STRUCTURING FACILITIES

The individual items of data in a database do not exist in isolation; they are related in some way. For example there is a relationship between a person's name, height, age, weight and sex. These are related items and can be grouped together.

Sometimes the relationships are more complex. A person may own several cars, or even a string of racehorses. There is a one-to-many relationship in such a case. In another case a group of people in partnership may own a fleet of cars. This gives a many-to-many relationship between the details of the people and the details of the cars. Each person is the part-owner of a number of cars, and each car is owned by a number of people.

Identification of the fundamental groups of data and their relationships is called data modelling. The process is independent of any computer implementation. Data modelling is the first stage in designing a database. If it is not done properly before the database is implemented, some of the benefits will be lost. Moreover, changes will be difficult, or even impossible, to accommodate.

Any DBMS must provide adequate facilities to allow these natural relationships to be implemented. The ease or otherwise of implementing the data model can significantly affect the effort required to design the database and develop application systems.

Simple normalised structures can be implemented very easily in relational systems. The order example in the chapter on normalisation resulted in four relations or tables: ORDER, SUPPLIER, PRODUCT and LINE ITEM. The relational model for this order data is straightforward, and in third normal form is:

> ORDER (Order Number, Date, Supplier Number, Order Total Price)
>
> SUPPLIER (Supplier Number, Supplier Name, Supplier Address)
>
> PRODUCT (Product Number, Product Description, Product Price)
>
> LINE ITEM (Order Number, Product Number, Product Quantity, Product Total Price).

It converts directly into four tables. The links between these four tables are the key attributes, Order Number, Supplier Number and Product Number.

The structure can be represented as shown in Figure 4.1.

Notice that the attributes used to link tables need not always be keys in those tables. For instance Supplier Number is a Key in SUPPLIER, but not in ORDER. It would be usual to define attributes used for linking on the same domain. Thus Supplier Number would be defined on the same domain throughout the database.

This first diagram does not show the complexity of the structure that is implicit in these tables. Each ORDER tuple has a one-to-many relation with LINE ITEM tuples. There is a one-to-one relation between an ORDER tuple and a SUPPLIER tuple, and similarly there is a one-to-one relation between a LINE ITEM tuple and a PRODUCT tuple. Looking in the reverse direction things are not so simple. Each SUP-PLIER tuple has potentially a one-to-many relation with ORDER tuples. Similarly a PRODUCT tuple has a one-to-many relationship with LINE ITEM tuples.

This structure is incorporated in the database almost without us being aware of it. There is no need to define access paths in advance. All useful access paths between data items can be established by suitable use of the relational operators project, select and join.

There are no pointers in a relational model. It is the key values that provide the linkage paths between tables.

James Martin in *Computer Data-Base Organisation* (1977) points out that it sometimes comes as rather a shock to the database specialist

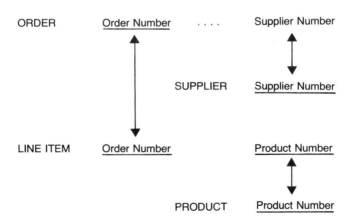

Figure 4.1   Relationships of Key Attributes

steeped in tree and plex structures to hear that *all such structures can be represented as flat files*.

It is clear that appropriate normalisation techniques can reduce any set of data to third normal form. From this one can construct a relational model. The process of normalisation may involve adding extra fields to a data record so that the key is unique. At first sight a normalised definition seems to have more fields than the original set. For instance the original order form example had eleven items of data ranging from order number to order total price. Admittedly some of these were repeated. The third normal form of the same data has fourteen items of data. The three extra ones are the keys used to link the three new relations. These each appear in two tables.

First appearances are deceptive. The normalised form of the data will probably occupy less space in practice, because the supplier and product data will occur once only for each different supplier and product. In the unnormalised form the data was repeated for each order and line item.

We see then that the representation of structure will involve adding keys to some tuples to represent links that might be shown by pointers in other database systems. Certain paths may not be represented unless additional attributes are included.

A relational database would normally be designed from the outset so that data items can be added. When new applications or the user view

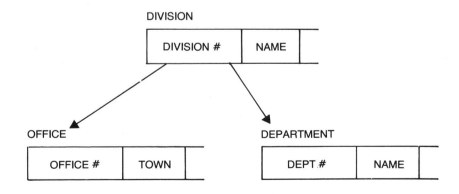

Figure 4.2 Division Structure

requires changes, new links can be added between tuples in pairs of tables. For example one could have a division with several departments and several offices (Figure 4.2).

The relational normalised form of this is:

DIVISION (DIVISION#, NAME, . . .)

OFFICE (OFFICE#, TOWN, . . .)

DEPARTMENT (DEPT#, NAME, . . .)

Suppose that we want to show which departments are located in which offices. Suppose further that offices can house several departments. All we need in the relational scheme is an additional relationship LOCA-TION showing OFFICE# and DEPT# thus:

LOCATION (OFFICE#, DEPT#)

The relational select can be used on this to pick off either which offices house a given department or set of departments, or which departments are housed in a given office or set of offices. Thus plex structures can be represented quite simply in the relational system. Most of the links shown on diagrams in conventional schemes represent relations of degree 2 between two domains as in the office# department# example above.

Sometimes designers draw directed arrows on such diagrams, implying pointers from one data item to another item or set of items. Such one-way or even two-way paths are often inflexible. They frequently represent not connections between the data in the logical model, but connections in the physical representation of the data model. Martin says that *lines with arrows offer the designer of the logical database the temptation to draw structures which are inflexible, misleading and sometimes invalid.*

Codd draws attention to the 'connection trap' that occurs when lines are used to link from one block to another, and from that to a third. The user tends to follow from the first item to the third one, and to assume that a ternary relation exists between them. The temptation is to represent such connections by a binary relation. Consider the case shown in Figure 4.3.

The user may conclude from the arrows that Product 5 is made from

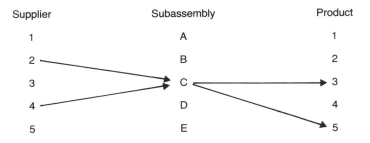

Figure 4.3   Supplier/Subassembly/Product Relations

subassemblies C that are supplied by supplier 4. He may be right or wrong. Ternary relations are needed to clarify the situation which may be Case 1 or Case 2 (Figure 4.4) or indeed several others.

Case 1				Case 2		

Supplier	Subassembly	Product
2	C	3
2	C	5
4	C	3
4	C	3

Supplier	Subassembly	Product
2	C	5
4	C	3

Figure 4.4   Possible Ternary Relations

The fact that subassembly C is a common mode in the network does not mean that the paths necessarily join at that point. Incidentally if the relation was important we could define it, in the database, as a ternary relation.

How about tree structures on the same class of objects such as a management tree? How can this be represented in a relational system?

One might define a table RS (reporting structure) connecting each employee with his manager using employee number E# from a common domain:

RS (EMP – E#, MGR – E#)

This shows for each employee (EMP–E#) his manager's employee number (MGR–E#). Both attributes of the table are drawn from the domain of employee numbers, E#. Each tuple is a link between an employee and his manager. In any tree structure like this there are certain limitations:

— no employee is his or her own manager. We could assert that in RS, EMP–E# ≠ MGR–E#;

— no employee has more than one immediate manager;

— if x is the immediate manager of y, then y cannot be the manager at any level of x. This would imply a loop.

Relational systems are a bit ragged in this area at the moment. Tree structured retrieval is relatively easy in domain relational calculus. Query-By-Example has facilities for this purpose. Two examples are shown:

1   Get the employee number for every employee four levels below E17 in the reporting structure.
Range of EX is E#
EX where EMP (EMP# (4L) = EX, MGR# = E17)

2   Get employee numbers for employees
     a) below E17 anywhere in the tree, that is all the people in E17's group or division
     b) at the lowest level below E17, that is those furthest in rank below
     c) those below E17 with no one reporting to them, who do not manage or supervise anyone else.

Tree structure implies ability to respond to queries such as these. It is also necessary to be able to determine relative levels in a hierarchy, between any two items. Query-By-Example has suitable facilities, but they are not universal. The essential problem in relational systems is not that of representing such relationships, but of controlling them to maintain the integrity. Much can be done by assertions, which are used to constrain values in the database. These are discussed in Chapter 7.

Bill of materials is another tree-structure problem. In engineering the products made by a factory are made up from small components such as nuts and bolts. These are joined up to make minor components. In turn these components are assembled to make subassemblies. There may be five or six levels in this process. The various bits and pieces that go to make a product are listed in a bill of materials, that shows the breakdown of the product level by level (Fig. 4.5).

There will usually be links from one level to other levels below the immediate inferior. Most products will contain some parts, for instance. The complex structure that results can be reduced to two relationships when properly normalised in the relational system:

ITEM (ITEM#, CATEGORY, NAME)

BREAKDOWN (ITEM#, COMPONENT-ITEM#, QUAN-TITY)

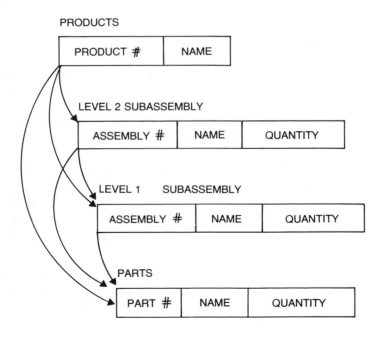

Figure 4.5   Assembly Levels

For each item, whether product, subassembly or part, we have an entry in Item, with Key Item#. The build or breakdown of this item is given in a set of records in Breakdown, linked with Key Item#. The second field, Component-Item#, is needed to form a unique key for the record, since Item# on its own would not suffice. Such a relational scheme can incorporate any complexity of build.

Engineering modifications to a bill of materials are very common. Such changes can be included very easily by simple manipulation of the two tables. A record of which items are affected by a change could be maintained in a third file linked by Item# to the first two files.

Relational systems can easily support quite complex logical structures. The structure is a function of the actual data, rather than the physical representation.

It is relatively easy to navigate through a relational structure, because the map and signposts are given by the data. In other words, the user who knows the data can derive all useful results through the relational operations.

DATA INDEPENDENCE

Data independence is another important aspect. It means that the physical or logical structure of the data can be changed without changing the data that is seen by the application programs. The level of data independence provided by a DBMS is very important. Much of the benefit of database stems from data independence.

In a conventional system each program using a file contains the definition of the format of the record type or types held on the file. The program logic also makes assumptions about the structure of the file. The program may depend upon the sort sequence of the file for correct functioning. If the file is unnormalised, perhaps with multiple record types, the program is likely to reflect this structure. Consider things like batch header details, or repeating groups in conventional files.

If the format of such a file is changed in any way, all the programs using it will have to be examined, and probably altered. If for instance a new field is added, every existing program that uses the file will need maintenance, whether or not it uses the new field.

Even if the length of an existing field is changed, all the programs will probably need maintenance. Clearly programs that use the field will be directly affected. Their logic will need to be checked. Unfortunately all the others will need to be changed. For example if a record is transferred to a work area, the definition of the work area will have to be changed to match the new definition. And so it goes on.

Three types of data independence are recognised:

— *Device Independence*. Programs are independent of the physical devices on which the data is stored. DBMSs usually provide device independence as a matter of course;

— *Physical Data Independence*. Programs are independent of the way in which data is physically organised. This implies that it should be possible to change the physical position of the records in the database, without affecting the programs. It should also be possible to change the physical format of the data, say from decimal characters to binary or vice versa;

— *Logical Data Independence*. This allows the logical structure of the data to be changed without affecting the application program's view of the data. It should be possible to change the record structure, by adding new fields, or reordering existing fields. Their sizes might be changed, and unused fields could be deleted.

Relational systems provide a great deal of data independence. Physical data independence is almost implicit in the relational approach. The order of the records in a table is indeterminate, because the records are an unordered set. The physical order of the fields or attributes is hidden from the user. An application may specify a particular order of presentation. This need not correspond to the physical implementation. One can add an attribute to a table without affecting existing relational processing programs. For instance, one could have a relation Supplier:

SUPPLIER (Supplier Number, Supplier Name, Supplier Address)

One could add a new field to such a table, say Supplier Phone:

SUPPLIER (Supplier Number, Supplier Name, Supplier Phone, Supplier Address)

Such a change would not affect a typical SELECT acting on this relation, for example:

SELECT Supplier Number, Supplier Address

FROM   SUPPLIER

WHERE   Supplier Number = 1234;

We might later find that Supplier Phone was no longer needed and that no programs used that field. One could eliminate it (perhaps by PRO-JECTION) and not affect any programs.

Data independence can be maintained even in host language support environments, where the relational system is interfaced with a conventional programming language such as COBOL or FORTRAN.

The host language programs are presented with a record generated from the relational system. The usual relational techniques are used to retrieve a table containing the desired records. These are then presented one-by-one to the host language program, perhaps ordered on some field or fields.

The record that is presented to the host language need not be affected by underlying changes in the tables in the relational system.

The project facility gives exceptionally good data independence, since it specifies which particular attributes are wanted. Fields that are not mentioned are automatically ignored. For instance one could project a table ORDERVALUE from ORDER:

ORDER (Order Number, Date, Supplier Number, Order Total Price)

PROJECT ORDERVALUE (Order Number, Order Total Price)

We could add or delete fields from ORDER without affecting ORDERVALUE table, unless of course we delete one of its two attributes from the ORDER table.

5 Access Control

The database approach means that an organisation keeps its data as a corporate resource. There should be one logical copy of any item of data. Consequently various users will have access to the database to help them in their duties.

A typical example is the use of personnel data. One would expect the organisation to keep one set of data on its personnel. Unfortunately some of the information on such a personnel record is sensitive, in the sense that neither the organisation nor the individuals concerned would want to allow completely open access to it. Other corporate data is sensitive for different reasons. There is a need to control access to the data so that only certain people can read it.

Control is also needed on other kinds of access. If a person's salary is defined by a field somewhere in the database, it might be unwise to allow that person to change it. One might still allow them access for reading it, but deny write access.

In a relational database this means that the system must be capable of enforcing certain access control rules. The personnel file might be represented as relational tables. It could include various attributes for each employee, including name, address, date of birth, next of kin, manager reference, job title, salary, etc. It could include performance assessment. If the record is comprehensive the access control problems may be formidable. One might allow an employee to have read access to most of his own record. This means that the database system should allow him to select only a part of his record, and deny him access to anyone else's. Managers may need to view the records for their own staff. Probably managers might be allowed to see a different set of attributes. They might update the assessment attribute, but not other fields. A salaries officer could be given access to change the salary of any employee, but not to see many other fields on the records. Furthermore, one might impose constraints on the amount of any change and on the maximum salary, but these are aspects of security other than of access control.

One of the most elegant techniques for defining such access requirements is the concept of a *view* of the database. Suppose that the salaries officer is allowed to access the employee number (E#), the employee name (NAME) and salary (SALARY). One could *project* a view of the actual relation so that in effect he sees only these three attributes. His view includes no other attributes, and is a projection from the main database. One could define a different view for the employee by a suitable combination of selection and projection. Again the view for a manager could be defined as a selection of the records for those staff who report to him. We can protect sensitive data by simply excluding it from the view defined for that user. The effect is that the data does not exist in that user's view, so he cannot access it at all.

A collection of definitions of such views of the database forms a powerful tool. In SQL syntax the salaries officer view might be defined as:

    DEFINE VIEW SALOFFICER

    AS SELECT E#, NAME, SALARY

    FROM EMPLOYEE

In SQL a reserved word USER is available to indicate the current user. If the user is the manager, his view of his own staff could be defined as:

    DEFINE MYEMPS

    AS SELECT *

    FROM EMPLOYEE

    WHERE DIV#=(SELECT DIV#

        FROM DIVISION

        WHERE MGR#=USER)

Here we use the relation DIVISION (DIV#, MGR#) to confirm the manager's identification with the employees in his division.

Various shades of access can be identified, especially where we need to control access according to the value of attributes within the database. At the simplest level we can grant or deny access to an attribute of the base relation. We can allow access according to the value of some attribute or attributes, using selection criteria to define the view. This is the case in the division manager example. We might allow access to information about particular predefined classes of information, or wish the access to be controlled dynamically at execution time. The difference is important. Fixed rules can be compiled into the access programs, but dynamic ones, that depend upon the data, must be checked during execution.

The user can be granted different levels of access (SELECT, UPDATE etc) to different subsets of the same table. An employee might be allowed to read all the data on a customer file, but only be permitted to update data for customers in a particular region or territory. Two views would be needed.

When a record is inserted through a view into a base table some attributes in the base table may not exist in the view. These will generally be set to null, but a mechanism for generating default values would be valuable.

SQL has two statements GRANT and REVOKE to define access privileges to users. There are six privileges that apply to tables: SELECT, UPDATE, DELETE, INSERT, INDEX and EXPAND. INDEX allows a user to create an index on the table and EXPAND allows him to add a new field. The whole collection of six privileges can be referenced as ALL PRIVILEGES. For programs and program-like objects there is a RUN privilege. There is a special RESOURCE privilege, which allows creation of new tables. This is originally the preserve of the database administrator who has another special DBA privilege. The two operators GRANT and REVOKE are then used to grant access to various system objects and resources. The basic format is:

GRANT privileges ON object TO users
so that we may write:

GRANT SELECT ON EMP TO SMITH

GRANT UPDATE, SELECT ON PRODUCT TO JONES

The word PUBLIC can be used to grant all users a particular access privilege:

GRANT SELECT ON SUPPLIERS TO PUBLIC

It is possible to hand down the GRANT power to another user, so that he in turn can define the access allowed to an object. REVOKE is used to deny access privileges already GRANTed.

The various privileges granted are held in tables, so that they can be accessed with SQL statements by the database administrator.

In Query-By-Example access is controlled by forms of authorisation constraint. The constraints are P., I., D. or U. (Print, Insert, Delete or Update), and they are inserted on a blank table in typical Query-By-Example fashion, after calling up the table, say PRODUCT:

PRODUCT		P#	NAME	SIZE
I AUTH (P.,I.)	BROWN	_PX	_NAME	

This would give BROWN print and insert authority on P# and NAME in table PRODUCT.

It is relatively easy to devise schemes that permit quite complex levels of control on access. It is difficult to be sure that the control provisions are logically correct, if they are complex. This is especially true where access is allocated to groups, and also to individuals. Revocation of individual access may still leave that individual with authority to access the resource through the group mechanism. For example, we might have:

GRANT SELECT ON X TO BROWN

Later we add

GRANT SELECT ON X TO PUBLIC

Revoking the first command will not deny access to Brown. It may not be simple to see this in a practical case.

One good way of displaying access rules is the authorisation matrix, which could itself be a relation. One row is allocated to each user, and one column to each data or other object. The access modes permitted are indicated at each intersection:

	Object A	Object B	Object C
User 1	NONE	NONE	ALL
User 2	SELECT	NONE	SELECT, UPDATE
User 3	UPDATE	NONE	ALL
User 4	ALL	ALL	NONE

Codd proposed a testing sequence to consider the validity of a request R (i,j) from some user i for some type of access to object j. The idea is that some highly privileged program would consider the request and grant or deny it. This program is called the *arbiter*. The test sequence is designed so that the arbiter can reach a decision most economically. Thus the earliest tests are the simplest, and the complex tests are deferred to later in the sequence. As soon as a test yields a 'yes' answer the decision is made, and later tests in the sequence are not necessary.

The first six tests are value independent and can be done at compile time. Tests 7 and 8 are value dependent. Those who have to implement access control mechanisms could well use the test sequence proposed to influence the way they establish access control paths. One should avoid value dependent constraints if other methods will suffice.

		Action if YES
Test		
1	Are all the relations mentioned in the request unconditionally accessible?	GRANT
2	Is there a relation mentioned in the request that is unconditionally prohibited?	DENY
3	Are all the attributes mentioned in the request unconditionally accessible?	GRANT
4	Is there an attribute mentioned in the request that is unconditionally prohibited?	DENY
5	Are all the attribute combinations mentioned in the request unconditionally accessible?	GRANT

6   Is there an attribute combination mentioned in the
    request that is unconditionally prohibited?   DENY

7   For each sensitive combination mentioned in the
    request is there a predicate that constrains the values of
    the participating attributes to lie within accessible
    ranges?   GRANT

8   Is there a sensitive combination in the request that has a
    subcombination whose values are permitted by the
    predicate to lie within a prohibited range?   DENY

If the response to all eight tests is negative, then the arbiter has
insufficient information to grant or deny the request.

Access control rules are important, but data can be revealed outside
the system. It is important to take a balanced, overall view, and not rely
totally upon the features of the DBMS.

6 Security and Integrity

SECURITY

The data that an organisation keeps on its database is of great value. Many business records may be held in the database. Relations with customers and suppliers may depend upon the database, and the applications built round it. Sales invoicing may be prejudiced if the appropriate parts of the database are not available. This could affect the cash flow of the business. Other aspects of customer relations can also be at risk. An organisation that provides field service for its machines or equipment may find that the quality of service will suffer if appropriate support is not available from the database. This could lead to loss of goodwill.

Secure means safe against attack or failure. The database is subject to both accidental and deliberate threats. The threat may cause loss of availability, integrity or confidentiality of the database. Loss of availability is a breach of security. As a consequence one cannot provide scheduled services at the proper time. The loss may be total or partial. None of the database applications may be available, or there may be a degraded level of service. This is a problem for any computer-based service. Essentially the problem is to maintain the database and everything that supports it in a fit state ready for use at all proper times.

The database contains a large amount of data. As a rule we expect that the data will be free from errors. Loss of database integrity means that the data is known to be in error or in some way incomplete. The database or parts of it could be lost or corrupted as a result of a hardware or software failure. A disk holding part of the database could become unusable or a rogue program could overwrite some of the files in the database. These kinds of failure are fortunately rare in modern systems.

Everytime the database is updated there is a risk that it could be damaged. The programs could leave the database in an inconsistent state. This is particularly true when the update involves changing data in several places at the same time so to speak. One of these items of data might be updated improperly so that it is inconsistent with the others. This might not become apparent until much later. Various techniques are used to maintain the integrity of the database, and to provide back-up and recovery when errors or losses occur.

The third aspect of security is maintaining confidentiality of sensitive information. Access control techniques (discussed in Chapter 5) are used widely to allow only authorised people to use and change the data. The spread of data protection laws to protect personal data means that confidentiality controls are of growing importance. Most regulations require the data user to apply proper security safeguards to protect against accidental or deliberate loss of data.

BACK-UP, RESTART AND RECOVERY

There are three main techniques for maintaining the integrity of the database: back-up, restart and rollback. These are intended to protect the database against the effects of malfunction in hardware or software. Various other techniques can be employed to exclude erroneous or inconsistent data. These are especially important in the relational systems, because so much relational processing depends upon being able to match attribute values in different tables. Techniques are discussed in the next section.

Back-up is a normal feature of any DBMS. The system includes utility programs which can copy the entire database onto another set of media. The database will usually be held on disk files. The back-up utility copies it to magnetic tape or to other disks. The utility needs to copy all the physical files at one time so that the copy is internally consistent. The process is called dumping, and takes a significant time for a large database. It must be done reasonably often. If the database becomes corrupt for any reason, the last dump can be restored. All the work that was done after the last dump will need to be rerun to bring the database up-to-date. Clearly frequent dumps will minimise this burden, but dumping itself occupies significant resources. The dump is a snapshot of the database at one point in time.

The DBMS usually maintains a log of all the changes made to the database. Sometimes this is called a journal or an audit trail. Usually the system copies a 'before' and 'after' image of each record that is changed. If there is a failure the 'after' images can be used to bring a previous dump up to date. This eliminates the need to rerun many hours of work. Clearly all the logs produced since the last dump are needed to accomplish this. The other technique is to use a DBMS utility to unwind the effect of a bad program using the 'before' image for all the affected records. The process is sometimes made automatic and called rollback. When an update program is active the system notes the before images of all the updated records in a special disk file. If the program fails, the DBMS uses these images to unwind the effects of that particular program. When the update program successfully completes its processing, its before images can either be discarded or added to the system log for possible use in a major recovery/restart sequence. Some DBMSs allow a program to invoke rollback of their own changes, if conditions make this appropriate. This is called back-out. Systems also maintain records of check points where the state of the database is known. The system can then apply rollback to particular checkpoints.

The data in a database is often shared between several applications. Such sharing does not present problems if all the programs only retrieve information. If some programs update the database there are two types of data inconsistency that can arise.

The first is *retrieval inconsistency*. This can happen if a program accesses an item of data twice, but another program updates the item between the two accesses. The integrity of the database is not destroyed but some strange results may occur. In a multi-user environment the programmer should not expect data to be unchanging if other users are allowed to update it. In a busy real-time system a second user may be able to update a record between two adjacent accesses by an enquiry user. Users should realise that this can happen.

The other problem is *update inconsistency*. If two programs attempt to update the same item of data at the same time there may be problems. Each program gets a copy of the data and updates it. The effect is that the first update will be lost, and the integrity of the database has been lost. Any self-respecting DBMS will protect against this kind of inconsistency by some kind of lock-out, or record holding strategies. Only one user will be allowed to access the item for update at one time. Unfortunately lock-out can bring further problems. Lock-out means that one user is given title to the record until his update is completed, and other users are denied access temporarily. Suppose that two users A and B both wish to update a pair of records, say X and Y. User A might grab record X while B grabs record Y. Neither can complete the sequence using the other record of the pair. This is known as deadlock, interlock or deadly embrace.

The usual solution is that the user should acquire update access to *all* the elements that need update in *one* operation. Thus A should have acquired X and Y, while B should have acquired Y and X. Usually DBMS can recognise the situation because two programs are held up. It can prevent deadlock occurring by insisting that users acquire title to all the items they wish to update in one command group. It could insist that they relinquish existing update accesses before asking for more, though this might be regarded as overkill.

So far as the user is concerned he deals in transactions. A transaction is a discrete unit of work. Either all of it should be done or none of it. A classical example is a transfer of funds between two accounts in a bank:

TRANSFER £123.45 FROM 84532109 to 14347628

The bank wants to apply both the credit and debit, or apply neither (for example account 84532109 may be out of funds).

The program that implements a transaction needs to begin the unit of work with a command like BEGIN TRANSACTION, and end it either with COMMIT or ROLLBACK. The COMMIT means that all the updates will be applied to the database, whereas ROLLBACK means that the system will leave the database unchanged by the transaction.

Transactions are an all-or-nothing proposition. In effect the system should provide a guarantee that if the transaction is executed, it is executed in its entirety, or that none of it is executed. The system should be a reliable transaction processor. It should process a user transaction exactly once. Transactions must not be lost, partially executed, or executed more than once.

Special precautions are needed if the system has to be recovered after a failure. Without such precautions the database may be left in a corrupt state. A transaction can be considered as a unit of recovery as well as a unit of work. This means that dumps of the system should be unique in terms of transactions, and that recovery processes or rollback processes should also operate in transaction units rather than simply field or record update units.

Rollback depends upon the log used to record the changes to elements of the database. The updates cannot be applied after a recovery without the log. If it is unavailable or corrupt, then work will be lost. Similarly the rollback is not possible unless the log is available.

Designers usually pay special attention to the security of dumping and logging systems. Dumps will usually be made in duplicate for instance. The log file or journal will be given special access protection, so that it cannot be changed like other files.

There is a practical point however. If a transaction is applied to the database it should be recorded in the log. This means that there are two distinct write operations, one to the database and one to the log. They are distinct. There is the possibility of failure between the two. One of the two is completed and the other is lost. If the survivor is the database update there is no record of it in the log. It cannot be undone. It follows therefore that the log details about the update should be recorded first, then the database updates should be done, and finally the transaction completion should be recorded in the log. If the system should break, the recovery system can then use the log and take special care with the transactions that are recorded as being in progress at the time of the break. The log has sufficient information to check the database images. This technique is called log write-ahead.

INTEGRITY RULES

In a relational system the attributes in any given relation can be defined on some domain. An employee number might be defined as a letter followed by three digits. This defines, at least partially, the domain for the attribute employee number.

The database system can incorporate facilities for specifying the domain values. Furthermore it could include automatic checks to ensure that the values supplied for each attribute did in fact conform to the rules for the associated domain.

The terms accuracy, validity and correctness are often used interchangeably with integrity in discussion of database systems. The database system might apply validation checks to transactions to ensure that the results matched any rules specified for the database.

Domain integrity rules are the simplest approach, though few systems have implemented them. In effect the system allows one to define the rules that apply for each domain used in the relations in the database.

Whenever an attempt is made to update a value or insert a value into the database the checks are applied. If the proposed value for an attribute would violate the rules for its domain various responses are possible. The simplest is to reject the proposed operation with an appropriate message. This would force rollback in a proper transaction system.

The domain rules could include all the usual validation checks on format, range, checks against lists of permitted values and so on. It is feasible to define rules for a data domain with day-month-year, which would apply the obvious rules such as $1 \leq month \leq 12$. The domain rules might also apply the rule 'thirty days hath September, . . .'. User defined rules are clearly feasible, especially for things like check characters.

The rules may also be defined in terms of values in the database. One could compare values before and after a proposed change. Such comparisons might involve other fields in the same record or elsewhere in the database. Rules of this kind are likely to impose an extra processing burden. They would allow a check of quantity ordered against a stock level for example. The pay-off in business terms may be worth the extra processing cost. Each case should be considered on its merits.

The various rules are called *constraints*. They can be classified according to how much access to information they need for implementation. Constraints that need no additional database access should be easy and cheap to implement. A constraint that involves examination of many other items in the database may be impossibly expensive to implement.

An important category is set constraint. Here we have to check the value against existing values of this attribute in this relation, probably for uniqueness. For instance one would not give two employees the same employee number. The check is clearly more expensive in processing time, especially if the set is large. Sometimes the value is a serial number and could be assigned automatically. Set values are vital from another angle. Key attributes must be unique, and the system should enforce this at minimum.

Integrity rules in relational languages are often specified by *assertions*. An assertion is simply a statement of something that we hold to be true, at least in the context under discussion. For instance we could assert that the quantity on hand in a table PART cannot be negative:

ASSERT A1 ON PART: QOH $\geq$ 0

This is an example of a tuple constraint.

One can have assertions on set values. For instance one could ensure that supplier references in GOODS-IN are in fact in the table SUPPLIER. The attribute is S# in each table:

ASSERT A2: (SELECT S# FROM GOODS-IN)

IS IN

(SELECT S# FROM SUPPLIER)

This is the SQL type of select, which is a project. We are insisting that S# in any GOODS-IN tuple is in fact in the set of all S# in SUPPLIER. The converse is not necessarily true: we do not assert that all suppliers are referenced in GOODS-IN.

One could use assertion to specify business rules that are to be applied in the database. For instance one might specify a minimum change in quantity-on-order in a table PRODUCT as, say, 100 units:

ASSERT ON UPDATE OF PRODUCT (QOO):

IF NEW-QOO > OLD–QOO

THEN NEW–QOO > 100+ OLD–QOO

The database model needs general machinery to define such constraints. People can usually define the rules that ought to be applied so that the system does not allow stupid mistakes to occur. It is usually much easier to prevent bad data from getting into the database than to correct it afterwards.

REFERENTIAL INTEGRITY

In the relational database system many operations depend upon the values of attributes in the tables. In a select operation the values of one or more attributes are commonly used to decide whether or not a record is included in the new table. In a join operation an attribute in the first table is matched with another attribute from the second table. The values used in such processes are often Key fields in the relations.

Keys are important in relational systems, so much so that special precautions ought to be taken to maintain the integrity of the values within Key fields.

Suppose we have two tables SUPPLIER, GOODS-IN:

SUPPLIER

S#	NAME	CITY
2	BROWN	PARIS
3	SMITH	TURIN
4	CANNON	NEW YORK

GOODS-IN

S#	P#	DATE	QYT
17	7	17.10.82	4
3	7	17.10.82	15
4	7	17.10.82	3
4	4	17.10.82	40

The GOODS-IN table shows some of the goods received from the suppliers shown in SUPPLIER. The references in these tables on supplier number, S#, are integers, but they are integers on a special domain, that of supplier number.

The attribute S# is the primary Key of the SUPPLIER table. We use it in the table GOODS-IN to reference the Supplier. The numbers in that table in column S# are references to supplier numbers in table SUP-PLIER. The number 3 refers to the supplier SMITH, and the two 4s refer to CANNON in NEW YORK.

The number 4 in the last line of GOODS-IN under P# does *not* refer to CANNON. It is on a different domain, part number, not supplier number.

What if the user requests deletion of the row with S# = 4 in the SUPPLIER table? Suppose that he realises that S# = 4 is used elsewhere in the database. How can we ensure that information is not lost from the database? How can we make certain that all the references to supplier number 4 are found and suitably modified? For example, we may want to change the reference number for S# = 4 to some new value. This means that all the references ought to be changed.

The system must keep track of which attributes are defined on which domains, and which are used as keys.

If the user wants to delete a key record such as that for CANNON there should be a DELETE KEY function which will follow-up all the references. Similarly there should be a CHANGE KEY function. In both cases the system should follow all the cascades from the specified key value.

Constraints like this are necessary if the relational system is to operate correctly. The necessary constraints should be embodied in the system so that the integrity of the model is maintained. Without such constraints it is very easy for the database to degenerate into garbage.

7 Relational Database Technology

GENERAL

The relational approach makes it possible to express queries in very simple ways. Even complex queries on large databases can be formulated quickly. The objects being manipulated are files, rather than records. The implication is that a lot of processing capacity may be needed.

People have objected to the relational approach because it could not be supported effectively by existing technology. Features like relational join require a great amount of processing for any but trivial files. The problem is much like sorting. It is easy for small files, hard for big ones and nearly impossible for very large ones.

Great improvements have been made in the computation techniques used to implement relational operations. Optimisation strategies are used to economise on the processing needed to implement queries.

CONTENT ADDRESSABLE DEVICES

The major problem for the implementation is that the relational database is *content addressed*, rather than *position addressed*. A record or tuple is identified by its content, especially its key, rather than by its physical or logical position. An operation like SELECT usually involves one or more attribute (field) values of the records. A large number of records need to be processed to select the ones that are needed. The amount of data that must be processed can be very large.

However, there is nothing in the rules that prevents the system from holding an index showing where various records are held. If a particular table has a certain key then the system could keep internally an index showing where various key values are held. The system can then access records with particular key values more quickly. Techniques of this sort are widely used to improve performance.

The relative reduction in hardware cost has made possible new devices. Associative memories may become widely available in the next few years. Some are already available. Microelectronics advances suggest that costs are likely to tumble as the market grows.

Storage devices like disks provide a major problem for database technology, because access is so slow. In a conventional system a disk pack can have twenty or more magnetic surfaces where information is stored. The pack is mounted on a drive, and rotated at perhaps 3000 rpm. The disk drive is connected to the processor through a disk controller.

Within the drive there is an assembly of read/write heads, with one head per surface. The assembly can be moved as a unit so that the heads are positioned at various points across the rotating surfaces. Each position is called a track, and there may be several hundred tracks on each surface. The head assembly moves as a unit so that all the heads are positioned over the same relative track on their own surface. The set of corresponding tracks is called a *cylinder*. It consists of all the tracks with the same relative track number, one track from each surface of the pack. If the surfaces have say 200 tracks, and there are 20 surfaces, then there will be 200 cylinders and each cylinder will have 20 tracks in it. The important thing is that the disk controller can read and write information anywhere inside the cylinder within one revolution of the disk. Since each surface has its own read/write head, any item in the cylinder can be accessed. Unfortunately all the other information in the disk is inaccessible without moving the head assembly to another cylinder. This is called a seek, and is quite slow, even on very good disk drives.

The implications of this are very significant for a relational database system, especially if it is large. The disk is a very position dependent device. Information is accessed by its position within the disk pack. If we know the location of the information, we can find it. More significantly the performance of the disk will improve if we arrange to access data in order, rather than arbitrarily. If we ask for 100 items from one cylinder access will be much faster than if we ask for 100 items from various places on the disk.

Relational systems are content addressed, not position addressed. The route to an item of information is determined by its key. We might have to examine thousands of tuples or records to find those with the wanted key.

Associative disk stores may provide a solution. The ICL CAFS (Content Addressable File Store) is one example. Extra hardware is interposed between the controller and the disk drive. This contains a number of selector-storage units. The details of a wanted record (the keys) are placed in a selector. There are several selectors each holding the key for a different record. The disk is then arranged to scan cylinder by cylinder, so that all the data is fed past the selectors, record by record. Each selector is searching for a record that satisfies its own key. As soon as it finds a suitable record it passes it to the main processor, and accepts another search key.

Two things should be noticed. The first is that traffic to the main processor is very much reduced, since only wanted records have to be passed. The other is that search time is much faster, because there are several parallel searches being handled by the several selector units. Also the seeks of the hardware can be controlled automatically without needing to pass address information from the main processor to the disks.

It is feasible to search the entire contents of a disk pack (several hundred megabytes) in a few seconds. Not only that but several access requests can be serviced in parallel during one pass over the disk pack.

At present such devices are quite expensive, but clearly micro technology could dramatically reduce costs, and improve the throughput of such systems.

THE DATABASE MACHINE

There have been several proposals for a database machine, since conventional architectures are not ideal for a dedicated DBMS environment. A problem is that people want the best of both worlds. They want the flexibility of a general-purpose system, but they also want high performance from the DBMS.

There is a severe mismatch between the capabilities of a conventional system and the needs of a DBMS. This is again because the conventional system is position addressed, whereas the database needs content addressing. The result is that the index files, pointers and so on, may occupy more space than the real data. Retrieving what seems to be a simple item of data may need many accesses to the files before the actual item can be found.

There is no general agreement about what constitutes a database machine. One approach considers it as specialised hardware supporting basic DBMS functions. Other people reserve the term to mean a storage device that incorporates some new hardware technology. There are two approaches. One, finding uses for the newer technologies and the other, enhancing the performance of moving-head technologies. It seems probable that we shall see a convergence in this area. Newer devices will be absorbed into existing architectures rather than displacing them completely.

The first commercial database machine appears to be the ADABAS Database Machine which supports ADABAS running on an IBM 370 compatible machine. It runs a specially streamlined version of the operating system, and carries up to eight copies of the ADABAS software. A single machine can be connected to several mainframes; equally one mainframe could have several database machines connected to it.

Britton Lee, Inc, produced the IDM 500 (the Intelligent Data Machine). This is a hybrid machine with a special processor running the DBMS and an associative disk store. The query input to the system is similar to SQL but must be in a special format. The Britton Lee machine can be connected to a normal conventional host or it can be accessed through a programmable terminal. The reason is that the interfaced machine has to do part of the work. Specifically it has to do the following things:

— accept the user request in a language like SQL and transform it into an IDM language called IDL;

— send the request to the IDM and accept the response;

— translate the response into a format acceptable to the user.

The IDM can support up to 32 billion bytes of on-line data. It can achieve transaction rates of 20-30 per second.

Is is suggested that relational systems require some kind of hardware breakthrough. There is no reason to suppose that a relational system implemented on conventional hardware would perform any better or any worse than any other kind of database. It may be much easier to specify a complex query in a relational system than in other systems. The time taken to service the request could well be the same.

It seems likely that additional hardware will be used to bridge the gap between the storage devices used in conventional systems. Mainframes now have huge main immediate access storage, measured by yesterday's standards. The next level of storage – typically multi-surface disk technology – has also increased in size. The relative access speed is still much as it was. Associative stores might well act as a buffer between the two. The demand for better performance is always with us.

Section 2

REPRESENTATIVE SYSTEMS

8 Structured Query Language (SQL)

INTRODUCTION

The SQL/Data System is one of IBM's relational database management products. It can be run on any 370, 43xx, 30xx or compatible mainframe running one of the virtual storage operating systems such as DOS/VSE, VM but not MVS.

SQL has all the features expected in a DBMS which has to support a variety of applications and operational environments. It has a high-level language interface, called the Structured Query Language, which supports data definition and manipulation. The DBMS supports multiple users with appropriate integrity controls to prevent concurrent update of the same data. Data integrity is further protected by its logging facilities which support automatic recovery in the event of an application or system failure. A flexible password controlled access mechanism allows users' access rights to the data to be carefully defined. The following sections of this review of SQL will describe each of these facilities in more detail.

THE LANGUAGE INTERFACE

The Structured Query Language (SQL) consists of high-level data definition and manipulation commands which may be entered into the system together in three different ways. SQL commands may be entered directly at a display terminal (VDU) through the use of the Interactive SQL Facility which runs as an on-line transaction under the teleprocessing monitor known as CICS. Commands may also be entered as batch input to SQL's Data Base Services Utility program, thereby providing a report writing capability. The third way in which SQL commands can be used is

109

as embedded requests for data within batch or on-line application programs. These application programs may be written in COBOL, PL/I, FORTRAN or Assembler language.

The major query, data manipulation and data definition commands will now be described. These are summarised in Figure 8.1. The function of each command is then explained in sufficient detail to give the reader an idea of the power of the language. In addition to the commands discussed below there are commands to define access rights and other control facilities.

Query Command	
SELECT	Retrieves data from one or more tables
Data Manipulation Commands	
INSERT	Adds one or more rows into an existing table
UPDATE	Changes data in one or more rows of a table
DELETE	Removes one or more rows from a table
Data Definition Commands	
CREATE TABLE	Defines the structure of a new table to SQL
DROP TABLE	Removes the definition of the table from the system
ALTER TABLE	Adds a new column to a table definition
CREATE INDEX	Allows a table to be indexed on one or more columns
DROP INDEX	Removes the index from the system
CREATE VIEW	Defines a user view of part of the database
DROP VIEW	Removes the view from the system

Figure 8.1   Major Query, Manipulation and Definition Commands

The Query Command

SELECT

SQL has only one powerful query command for retrieving data from one or more tables. This is the 'SELECT' command which has the form:

SELECT   identified-data

FROM   table-name-or-names

WHERE   optional-selection-criteria

ORDER BY   optional-ordering-of-the-selected-data

The simplest form of query which will display a whole table is:

SELECT * FROM table-name

The number of rows of data retrieved can be controlled by specifying a condition which must be satisfied by the data in the rows for it to be retrieved. This condition may be a compound logical statement using the data values held in the tables:

SELECT * FROM table-name

WHERE col1–name = value [AND col2–name = value]. . .

If only a few of the columns in the table are required these may be selected by name:

SELECT col1–name, col2–name, . . . FROM table-name

WHERE etc

The optional ORDER BY clause allows the result to be produced in ascending or descending sequence on one, or a combination of columns:

SELECT * FROM table-name

ORDER BY col1–name, col3–name DESC, col6–name

The examples used above only refer to one table. SQL enables data from more than one table to be selected in two ways. One way, termed a subquery or nested query, places one query within another as illustrated below:

SELECT col1–tab1, coln–tab1 FROM table1–name

WHERE colm–tab1 = (SELECT colx–tab2 FROM table2–name
WHERE condition)

In this example, data is retrieved from table1 but the rows are only selected if colm values in table1 appear in the corresponding colx in table2 for rows in table2 which satisfy the 'condition'. Clearly colm in table1 and colx in table2 will generally have a common meaning for the request to make any sense.

The second way of selecting data from more than one table is called the joining method. This allows data held in a number of tables to be presented to the user as just one table tailored to that user's requirements. The condition in the WHERE clause identifies how the tables are linked in order to perform the join.

SELECT   colm–tab1, coln–tab1, colx–tab2, coly–tab2, colz–tab2

FROM   table1–name, table2–name

WHERE   coln–tab1 = colz–tab2

Data Manipulation Commands

The data manipulation commands are used to insert, update and delete data from the tables in the SQL database. The tables must have been previously defined to the system by means of the data definition commands (described later).

INSERT

The INSERT command is used to add new rows into a table. The values to be inserted must be in the same order as the columns in the table.

INSERT INTO table-name

VALUES (val1, ... valn)

Data may be inserted or merged into one table from another similar table as follows:

INSERT INTO table–name: SELECT clause

Large volumes of data can be added by means of the Data Base Services utility. Medium volumes of data can also be input in a tabular format. The INSERT command is usually used for very small volumes of additions.

UPDATE

The UPDATE command is used to change one or more values in a table. One command can reference a number of columns in a table. A 'condition' can be used to identify which rows in the table are to be changed. The command has the following form:

UPDATE table–name

SET colm = value [,coln = value]. . .

WHERE condition

DELETE

The DELETE command removes one or more rows from a table. It has the following form:

DELETE FROM table–name

WHERE condition

All the rows satisfying the 'condition' are deleted from the table. If the WHERE clause is absent all the rows in the table will be deleted leaving an empty table. The table definition will still exist and rows could be inserted into it at a later date.

Other Data Manipulation Facilities

SQL/DS has a number of built-in functions for performing arithmetic calculations on the columns in a table. Examples are SUM, MIN, MAX, AVG and COUNT. The purpose of these is clear from their names. Null values are ignored. The example below will count the number of rows in the table which satisfy the 'condition'.

SELECT COUNT(*)

FROM table–name

WHERE condition

This example counts all rows in the table, including duplicates, since SQL does not require rows to be unique. The function 'COUNT UNIQUE' will ignore duplicate rows.

Some types of queries are incestuous and need to reference other rows in the same table in the WHERE clause. For example, it may be necessary to join a table with itself, in order to answer a question such as: *which accounts have the same amount debited from them as has been credited to other accounts?* To answer this query dummy variables V1 and V2 are appended to the table name so that it may be referenced twice:

SELECT   ACCOUNT–CODE, DEBIT

FROM   ACCOUNT–TAB V1, ACCOUNT–TAB V2

WHERE   V1.CREDIT = V2.DEBIT

It is often necessary to partition a table into groups of rows. For example, subtotals may need to be produced every time the value of a given column, or possibly a combination of columns, changes. This is equivalent to control break on a report.

SQL supports partitioning into groups by means of a GROUP BY clause and a HAVING clause. The GROUP BY clause identifies the column, or columns, to be used to control the breaks. The HAVING clause allows a condition to be placed on a partitioned group of rows.

The example below shows how these two clauses can be used to produce the summation of 'col2–name' for all groups of rows in 'table–name' with the same values in 'col1–name'. Only groups containing more than four rows are selected.

SELECT   col1–name, SUM (col2–name)

FROM   table–name

GROUP BY   col1–name

HAVING COUNT (*) >4

Data Definition Commands

The data definition commands are used to define (and remove) tables, indexes and views to SQL/DS. They define the structure and format of the database. The data manipulation commands and Data Base Services utility are used to load data into the tables.

CREATE TABLE

A table is defined to the system with a CREATE TABLE command. This gives the table a name and also names the columns which comprise the table. The type of data, ie whether it is INTEGER, FLOAT, CHARAC-TER etc, is also defined. However, there are no facilities for specifying constraints on the data which may be entered into a table such as range checks etc. It is possible to specify that given columns must have values, so that they are not 'null' when a row is inserted. This command has the following form:

CREATE TABLE table–name

    (col1–name   type [NOT NULL]

    [,coln–name   type [NOT NULL]]. . .)

The created table will not contain any rows until these are added by the INSERT command or by use of the utility. When the table is no longer required and all of its rows have been deleted its definition can be removed from the system by an appropriately authorised user by means of the 'DROP TABLE table–name' command.

CREATE VIEW

SQL supports 'views' of the database. A view allows the data to be presented to a user in a different way to its defined structure. This allows it to be presented to a user in a format which is natural and tailored to his requirements. Views also provide a convenient mechanism for restricting a user view of the data for security reasons. A view can restrict a user's access to particular columns. It can also restrict a user to the rows in a table which satisfy a particular condition; for example, personnel information for his own department only.

A view also allows data from more than one table to be joined and presented as one table to the user. Views may also be defined with virtual columns. These are columns whose values are calculated from other data in the underlying table(s). Views which are defined from more than one table can only be used in retrieval requests; any updates must be performed on the underlying tables. If a view, derived from one table, contains virtual columns then insert and delete commands cannot be used on it although the non virtual columns may be updated. Given these restrictions a view may be treated as if it is a table and may be referenced in various SQL commands.

A view is specified as follows:

CREATE VIEW view–name

[(viewcol1, viewcol2, . . .)]

AS SELECT select–clause

The SELECT clause allows a new table format to be specified by selecting the required columns from one or more tables and specifying which rows are to be included by specifying a suitable 'WHERE condition' clause. It also permits the ordering of the resultant rows to be defined. The column names used in the view may be the same as those which are used in the SELECT clause. Alternatively the names to be used in the view can be specified in the optional name list enclosed in brackets.

When a view is no longer required an authorised user may remove its definition from the system through the use of a 'DROP VIEW viewname' command.

ALTER TABLE

It is sometimes necessary to add an extra field to each row in a table in order to hold the data needed by a new application. SQL allows a table definition to be extended to include a new column. A newly added column will contain null values until data is entered by use of an UPDATE command.

The command takes the following form:

ALTER TABLE table–name ADD column–name data–type

CREATE INDEX

SQL has an option to index a table in order to improve the performance of the system. There is no requirement to have any indexes for SQL to work. If indexes are used they are transparent to the users, they are only used internally. They are provided to speed up access, whenever necessary, to large tables which might otherwise involve time consuming searches. Indexes are useful for heavily used access paths, especially if only a few rows from the table are being accessed. A table may be indexed on one or more columns and it may have a number of different indexes. The command has the following form:

CREATE INDEX index–name

ON table–name (col1–name [,col2–name]. . .)

If the index is no longer required it may be removed from the system by an authorised user by issuing a 'DROP INDEX index–name' command.

THE INTERACTIVE SQL FACILITY (ISQL)

ISQL provides display terminal users with on-line access to the SQL database. ISQL executes as a transaction under IBM's teleprocessing monitor CICS. A complete range of on-line support facilities are provided:

— direct entry of the SQL commands with the results either displayed at the terminal or printed on the main printer;

— bulk data entry into tables;

— HELP command;

— creation and execution of stored SQL commands including a macro or parameter facility;

— report formatting commands which support titling, data editing, subtotalling and totalling;

— an extract facility (described below).

ISQL includes an Extract Facility which allows data to be extracted from a DOS/VS DL/1 database and stored as tables in the SQL database. DL/1 is an IBM database management system which is not based on relational principles and is therefore generally considered to require greater expertise to use effectively. A detailed description of DL/1 may be found in the NCC publication, *Database Management Systems: A Technical Review* by Alan Mayne.

The extract facility allows an authorised person, usually a Data Administrator, to define what data can be extracted from the DL/1 database and how it is to be mapped into SQL tables.

Users can request data to be extracted under ISQL but the request is held and satisfied off-line by running the Data Base Services Utility.

THE APPLICATION PROGRAM INTERFACE

The Structure Query Language may be used by batch and on-line application programs. However, there are some special considerations which must be dealt with which require a few additional commands. These special considerations are:

— storage must be allocated in the program to hold the row (which is just like a record retrieved from a conventional file);

— the SQL commands must be converted into a format which is acceptable to the programming language compiler;

— some means of processing a table comprising many rows (of records) is needed so that one row at a time may be referenced.

Allocating and Using Storage

Storage for the data to be communicated to and from the SQL database is allocated by defining a special DECLARE section in the application program. The format of the row, or record, is defined for references in the program. The SQL SELECT command references the table and column names known to SQL and associates them with the defined record layout. The example below illustrates the principle for COBOL programs. The format is modified slightly to suit the syntax of PL/I, FORTRAN and Assembler which are also supported.

```
DATA DIVISION.
WORKING-STORAGE SECTION.
     EXEC SQL BEGIN DECLARE SECTION END–EXEC.
77   PROGFIELD1      PIC . . .      USAGE . . .
77   PROGFIELD2      PIC . . .      USAGE . . .

77   PROGFIELDN      PIC . . .      USAGE . . .
77   PROGFIELDVAL  PIC . . .      USAGE . . .
     EXEC SQL END DECLARE SECTION END–EXEC.
—    other program entries        —
PROCEDURE DIVISION
—    program code        —
     EXEC SQL SELECT col1, col2, . . . coln
     INTO: PROGFIELD1, PROGFIELD2, . . . PROGFIELDN
     FROM table–name
     WHERE coln = : PROGFIELDVAL END–EXEC.
—    other program code        —
```

When an application makes a request to SQL it needs to know whether that request was successfully completed and if not, why not. In order to establish this a Communications Area is copied into the application program which contains a status or return code which indicates the success or otherwise of the last command. If this code is zero the operation was performed as requested. If it is positive its value indicates some special condition has arisen such as no rows found or the end of the data has been reached. Negative values imply an abnormal condition.

The Preprocessor

The preprocessor is used to analyse the program source code, with its embedded SQL commands, before it is compiled in the normal fashion. Two functions are performed by the preprocessor. First, the SQL commands are converted into standard host programming language statements. SQL commands use the language CALL facility to interface with the SQL/DS main code using parameters and the Communications Area to identify the required service.

The second function of the preprocessor is to generate an 'access module' which is used to define the program's data and access requirements for SQL/DS. This 'access module' is stored in the SQL database and is subject to all the usual access controls. The preprocessor ensures that the user has the authority to access the requested data from the SQL database. Figure 8.2 illustrates how the preprocessor fits into the normal compilation sequence.

Processing a Table

The result of an SQL command will, in many cases, be a table containing a number of rows. In order to allow an application program to access a row at a time, just as it would read a record at a time, SQL uses the concept of a 'cursor'. This cursor is used to reference a row at a time. It is defined as part of the SELECT command and then used in OPEN, FETCH, DELETE, UPDATE and CLOSE commands. The following example illustrates its use but for clarity the EXEC SQL and END–EXEC statements have been omitted.

DECLARE cursor–name CURSOR FOR

SELECT col1, col2

FROM table–name WHERE coln=:PROG1NAME

To start using the resultant table:

OPEN cursor–name

To access the first/next row in the table:

FETCH cursor–name INTO : PROG1NAME,:PROG2NAME . . .

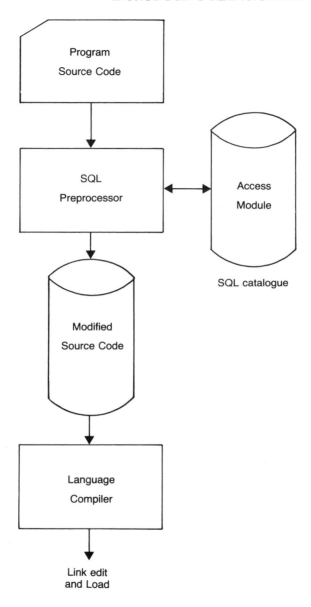

Figure 8.2 Normal Compilation Sequence and SQL Preprocessor

To update the current row in the table:

UPDATE table–name

SET colx=value

WHERE CURRENT OF cursor–name

To delete the current row from the table:

DELETE FROM table–name

WHERE CURRENT OF cursor–name

To signal completion of processing

CLOSE cursor–name

Dynamic Command Processing

The SQL commands described above are normally preprocessed and compiled into an application program. Some applications may wish to formulate the request at execution time. For example, a selection criterion may need to be specified as a parameter input at execution time. SQL allows this to be done through a dynamic command processing facility.

ACCESS CONTROL

To use the SQL database a user must first sign on by providing a valid user identification and its associated password. The authority of a batch program's access module determines whether it may access the database. The person responsible for SQL/DS security, possibly the Data Administrator, has the authority to maintain the user-ids and password information at any time.

Only appropriately authorised users may actually create new tables and preprocess programs. The creator automatically holds all the privileges to use the new object (an object being a table, view or access module). However, the creator can selectively share the object with other users by assigning them various 'privileges' or access rights.

A 'GRANT' command is used to assign privileges to another user and a 'REVOKE' command allows them to be taken away.

The privileges which apply to tables are SELECT, INSERT,

DELETE, UPDATE, ALTER and INDEX. The named privilege allows a user to use the similarly named command. Any combination of these privileges may be granted to another user. Different combinations may be granted to various users to suit their access requirements.

The owner of a table may even give other users the authority to GRANT access rights to another user! If a privilege is revoked from this user it is automatically revoked for lower levels of user. This prevents users who have been granted access rights indirectly from inadvertently being left with a privilege.

Access control down to the field level can be provided by granting users privileges on views of tables rather than the tables themselves. In a simple case the view can be a subset of a table containing only the columns to which access is to be granted. A view may also select rows from a table which satisfy a specified condition so a user can be given access to just those rows which are appropriate to his needs.

There are also a few special privileges which will generally be issued very selectively. The 'RESOURCE' privilege allows a user to create tables in the public DBSPACEs and acquire private DBSPACEs. A DBSPACE is simply a place where tables, views, etc are stored. Notice that the RESOURCE privilege is needed to create a table but users with the INSERT privilege can load data into the new table. The highest privilege is 'DBA' authority which permits read and update access to the whole database.

BACK-UP, RESTART AND RECOVERY

The Data Base Services Utility allows the database to be copied in order to create a back-up copy. The whole database must be copied as parts of the data cannot be selectively copied. Should the database be damaged or lost for any reason the back-up copy can be restored. Of course the restored copy may not be completely up-to-date.

SQL/DS also supports a logging facility which records all changes to the database. Both the pre-update and post-update copies are recorded. This log must be a disk file and if extra security against the failure of the log file is needed a duplex copy of the log may optionally be maintained.

The log enables automatic, or dynamic, backout of a failing program to be performed in order to maintain the integrity of the database. If a partially completed update sequence cannot be completed the data already updated is replaced by the pre-update copies held on the log. Automatic backout may be necessary if the program fails or if there is a conflict for access to data being updated by another program. A program may decide to initiate a rollback of itself as a result of a particular condition.

SQL/DS also writes checkpoint information to the log at regular intervals. At a checkpoint all completed changes are committed to the database and the appropriate status information is logged. In the event of a system failure, for example as a result of a power cut, SQL/DS knows what the state of the database was at the latest checkpoint. The log is used to roll forward the database from the latest checkpoint to include changes made by programs which finished after the checkpoint but before the failure. The system also rolls back the database to exclude changes made by any programs which had not finished. The net result of this is that all satisfactorily completed updates are recorded in the database but all partial updates are removed thereby maintaining the integrity of the database.

OPERATING ENVIRONMENT

SQL/DS can be run in single user mode or in multi-user mode. When it is used in single user mode the SQL software runs in the same partition or region as the user's application program.

In multi-user mode, SQL runs in its own partition or region. It waits for a request for database services from other programs within the computer. Logically, it can be considered as an extension of the operating system's data management software. The requests for service can come from any combination of batch applications, on-line transactions or from one of SQL/DS' own service programs. The communications between the application programs and SQL in another partition or region are handled by the operating system. An interface routine in the application's partition or region uses this operating system facility to communicate with SQL/DS. Figures 8.3 and 8.4 illustrate the organisation of the application code, interface routine and SQL/DS software.

MULTIPLE USER ACCESS AND LOCKING

As SQL/DS supports multiple user access it has a locking mechanism in order to maintain the integrity of the database by preventing concurrent update of the same data. SQL has two types of storage for holding tables, views and access modules. These are public and private DBSPACEs. The locking mechanism is different for each of these.

The objects which are held in a private DBSPACE can be concurrently read by any number of users who have the appropriate access rights. However only one user may update a private DBSPACE at any one time. If a request causes a conflict, ie one user wants to update while somebody else is reading it, or a user wants to read while somebody else is updating, then the request is not satisfied and an error code is returned to the requestor. In other words the whole of a private DBSPACE is exclusively locked for update.

Almost by definition, objects in a public DBSPACE are more likely to be used concurrently so the locking mechanism for this type of DBSPACE does allow concurrent update providing that this does not result in any conflicts. The unit of locking is defined when the public DBSPACE is allocated. This unit may be a table row, a page (a physical block of data usually comprising a few rows) or the whole DBSPACE. If the unit of locking is the whole DBSPACE it will behave just like a private DBSPACE. At the row or page level multiple updates and

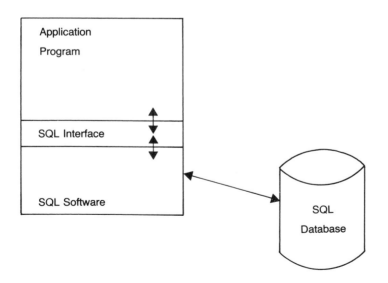

Figure 8.3   SQL in Single User Mode

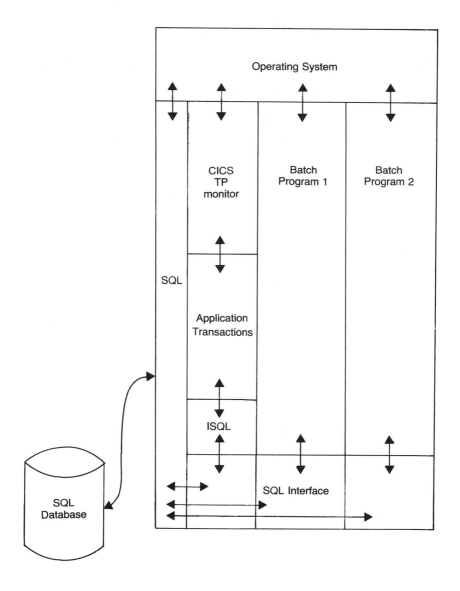

Figure 8.4   SQL in Multi-User Mode

retrievals can take place providing that the same rows or pages are not needed by different programs.

The programs place 'share locks' on the data that they read and 'exclusive locks' on the data they update. If a program needs to update a row which is in use by another program it is allowed to wait until the other program finishes with it. This could possibly result in a deadly embrace so SQL is designed to detect this situation and backout the youngest program which is involved.

All the data which a program accesses is 'share locked' and that which is updated is 'exclusively locked' until the program either finishes or signals through a COMMIT WORK command that an update sequence is complete. Notice that a share lock prevents a value being changed by another program thereby avoiding a situation where two different accesses to the same data return different values.

An update sequence which must be completed in order to maintain integrity is known as a logical unit of work. In many cases this will be an entire program or transaction. If the program or system fails, the database is recovered to the completion of the latest logical unit of work. This may be the beginning of the program unless a COMMIT WORK command has been issued in which case it will be recovered to the most recent COMMIT point.

9 Query-By-Example (QBE)

INTRODUCTION

Query-By-Example is an IBM produced data management system which runs under the VM/370 operating system. The product supports a relational database approach. Despite its name, QBE also permits update operations to be performed on the data and the table definitions themselves.

QBE is primarily an interactive query system designed for non-DP users. The QBE language is based on a graphic representation of tables of data. However, a linear syntax form of the language is available for batch use. Multiple user read access to a database (there can be many databases) is supported but concurrent update is not allowed. A log file is supported in order to assist in recovering a damaged database. Access rights to tables in a shared database may be controlled in a flexible manner. These aspects are discussed in more detail in the following sections.

THE LANGUAGE INTERFACE

The Query-By-Example language has been designed for interactive use at a visual display terminal. A graphic representation of tables is used in order to minimise the syntax of the language. The basis of this representation is a table skeleton which is used to define what operations are to be performed. A table skeleton has four types of areas as illustrated below.

table–name area	column–name area
row operator area	data entry area

127

The name of the table to be processed is entered in the 'table–name area'. The names of the columns being used are shown in the 'column–name area'. The 'row operator area' is used to specify what actions are to be performed against table rows. The 'data entry area' is used to specify column operators or actual data values.

The use of these areas is illustrated by means of examples below. Data definition and data manipulation commands are entered through the same language interface. For convenience these two aspects will be described separately. Other features of the QBE language are mentioned later.

Data Manipulation – Retrieval

In order to illustrate the data manipulation operators available we assume that a number of tables have already been defined to the system and that they have been loaded with data. The main retrieval operator is 'P.' for print or display. The following examples illustrate its use.

In order to print an entire table the following entry is made in the table skeleton:

table–name	col1–name	. . .	coln–name
P.			

The same result could be produced by using column operators instead of the row operator:

table–name	col1–name	. . .		coln–name
	P.	P.	P.	P.

Only the columns containing the 'P.' operator will be displayed so it is possible to display just a few selected columns. Alternatively unwanted column names could be deleted from the table skeleton (the stored table is unaffected) before using the 'P.' as a row operator.

The ordering of the displayed data may be specified as part of the 'P.' operator. 'P.AO' will sort the data into ascending order on that column while 'P.DO' specifies descending order. If more than one column is to be used as a sort key the order of the columns in the sort key is specified in brackets:

table–name	col1–name	–		coln–name
	P.AO(1)	P.DO(3)	P.DO(2)	

Usually a user is only interested in a small number of rows within a table. QBE allows selection criteria to be specified in the table skeleton. For example, to print the rows with a given 'value' in column 2 and values greater than say '100' in column 3 the entries would be:

table–name	col1–name	col2–name	col3–name	. . .	coln–name
	P.	P.value	P.>100		

The result produced by the above query will print the first three columns. However, all the entries in column 2 will be the same, in 'value'. If preferred this column could be omitted from the result by using the following query:

table–name	col1–name	col2–name	col3–name	. . .	
	P.	value	P.>100		

The examples used so far only display information from one table. Some requests require data from two or more tables to be combined in order to produce the result. Any two tables which have a column in common may be linked on that column. This means that a row in the first table is concatenated with all the rows in the second table which have the same value in the common column, in other words the tables are relationally joined.

In order to specify this action QBE uses what are termed 'example elements'. An example element is defined by an underscore character (_) followed by any numbers or characters. The numbers and characters simply identify the link. In the example below, the rows in table2 are displayed if the corresponding rows in table1 satisfy the condition.

table1–name	col1–name	col2–name		. . .	coln–name
	value	_AIXY			

table2–name	col1'–name	col2'–name	col3'–name	. . .	coln'–name
P.			_AIXY		

The result will be a subset of the rows of table2 (it could possibly be null or the whole of table2 depending upon the actual data values in the two tables). If table1 had a 'P.' operator in it too then two result tables would have been produced.

If required a new table may be created which comprises columns from two, or more, existing tables. The example below shows how two tables may be joined to produce a new table. This new table could, if required, be saved in the database.

table1–name	col1–name	col2–name	col3–name	. . .	coln–name
	_THIS	_ABC			

table2–name	col1'–name	col2'–name	col3'–name	. . .	coln'–name
	_NEEDED	_ANDTHIS	_ABC		

new–table–name	col1''–name	col2''–name	col3''–name
P.	_NEEDED	_THIS	_ANDTHIS

The resultant table comprises the first column of table1 and the first two columns of table2 produced by joining on a common column identified by the 'example element' _ABC.

The 'example element' may also be used to generate more complex queries which require linking between the rows of one table. For example, to find all the rows whose column 2 values are less than a given row identified by 'value' in column 1:

table–name	col1–name	col2–name	
	value	_LNK	
P.		<_LNK	

Arithmetic statements may also be used in columns so the above example could be modified to find all the rows whose column 2 values are less than the sum of the two rows identified by 'value1' and 'value2':

table–name	col1–name	col2–name
P.		$<(\_L1+\_L2)$
	value1	$\_L1$
	value2	$\_L2$

The use of arithmetic expressions also enables the creation of a new table which contains one or more columns calculated from one or more other tables. For example to print the sum of a number of columns the following query could be used:

table1–name	col1–name	col2–name	col3–name	col4–name
	$\_LNK$	$\_V1$	$\_V2$	$\_VAL3$

new–table	col1'–name	col2'–name	col3'–name
P.	$\_LNK$	$\_V1+\_V2+\_VAL3$	$\_V1*\_V2$

Data Manipulation – Modification

The data held in a table may be modified through the use of the insert operator 'I.', the update operator 'U.', and the delete operator 'D.'. The insert operator allows a new row to be added to a table. All the columns which uniquely identify the row, ie the key, must be provided but other columns may be left null. A newly inserted row appears at the end of the table.

table–name	col1–name	col2–name	col3–name	. . .	coln–name
I.	value1		value3		valuen
		/no value implies null/			

The update operator allows an existing row to be altered. Only columns which are not part of the key can be updated. If the key needs to be altered the row must be deleted and inserted so that the system can ensure uniqueness of the key. An update request must specify the key of the row to be altered and the new values for the columns to be updated:

table–name	col1–name (key)	col2–name	col3–name	. . .	coln–name
U.	value1	new–value	/no value no change/		

The update operator may also be used as a column operator so the above query could have been written thus:

table–name	col1–name (key)	col2–name	col3–name	. . .	coln–name
	value1	U.new–value			

If the key field is left blank on the update all rows in the table will be set to 'new–value'.

The delete operator allows one or more rows to be deleted from a table. It can be used to delete a specific row by specifying the key:

table–name	col1–name (key)	col2–name	col3–name	. . .	coln–name
D.	value1				

Alternatively it may be used to delete all rows which contain a given value within a column as follows:

table–name	col1–name (key)	col2–name	col3–name	. . .	coln–name
D.			value		

The delete operator may also be used to remove values from columns in one or more rows of a table by using it as a column operator. The deleted values are set to nulls. In the example below all the column 3 values are set to null if column 2 contains 'value'.

table–name	col1–name (key)	col2–name	col3–name	
		value	D.	

More sophisticated insertions and updates can be specified by using 'example elements' to reference data held in other rows of the table. For example, it is possible to insert a row and set selected column values based on the values in other rows:

table–name	col1–name (key)	col2–name	col3–name	
I.	value1	_L1 + _L2		
	value2	_L1		
	value3	_L2		

In the following example all values in a column are increased by 20%.

table–name	col1–name (key)	col2–name	col3–name	
	_ABC	U._S1*1.2		
	_ABC	_S1		

Deletes and updates may also be performed on a displayed table. The row operators D. or U. can be used. Updates are performed by altering the values displayed: (v represents any data value).

table–name	col1–name	col2–name	col3–name	. . .
	v	v	v	v
D.	v	v	v	v
	v	v	v	v
U.	v	new–v	v	v

The insert, update and delete operators define how the data in the tables is to be modified. A modification command is followed by a print command to display the altered table. The system then gives the user the opportunity to save the changes. A save causes the modifications to be written back to the database. If the user decides not to save the changes the database is left in its original state.

Other Data Manipulation Features

QBE supports the following built-in functions for counting and performing arithmetic functions on numeric data: CNT, SUM, AVG, MAX and MIN. The purpose of each of these is clear from its name. These functions may be qualified by 'UNQ' so that duplicate values can be omitted if appropriate. A 'group by' operator may be used in conjunction with these functions to produce a result every time the value in the group-by column changes.

A QBE retrieval request may be partially qualified by combining a constant and an example element. For example, if we wanted to display all the rows where a given column (which is of character format) starts with the letters 'AB', the retrieval query could contain 'AB'_EE. It is also possible to search for a character string within a column so all rows containing the string anywhere within the column are retrieved; such a string search is specified in the form _X'string'_Y.

The QBE language makes use of a Command Box and a Condition Box. The Command Box is used to direct output to a printer or disk file. It also allows a query to be stored and enables such a stored query to be executed. The Condition Box allows complex retrieval conditions to be specified. It may specify complex multi-column conditions as well as logical expressions. These two boxes extend the power of the language.

QBE supports an extract facility that allows data to be extracted from an IMS database. The extracted data is loaded onto a QBE database by the Bulk Loader utility.

Data Definition

A new table may be created during a terminal session provided that the database is being accessed in write mode. Before a new table is created some effort should be put into its design. Design involves deciding what data should go in which tables and considering what the keys are as well as which columns may be used to link tables together.

Creation of a new table starts by inserting the table's name, as well as the names of its columns, in a table skeleton:

I.table–nameI.	col1–name	col2–name	. . .	coln–name

The columns now have names and the system assigns them some default attributes. Other attributes, such as whether the column is to contain numeric or character data, must be specified in the next step of table creation. A list of the attributes may be printed using the query below.

table–name	col1–name	col2–name	. . .	
P.P.				

The resulting table is:

table–name	col1–name	col2–name	col3–name	. . .	
KEY	Y(DEF)	Y(DEF)	Y(DEF)	. . .	
DOMAIN	–	–	–	. . .	
TYPE	–	–	–	. . .	
IMAGE	–	–	–	. . .	
ICW	1 (DEF)	1 (DEF)	1 (DEF)	. . .	
POSITION	1	2	3	. . .	
INVERSION	Y(DEF)	Y(DEF)	Y(DEF)	. . .	

In this table 'DEF' means default. The KEY attribute specifies whether the column is to be part of the key for the row. A key field must be unique. The ICW, or Input Character Width, defines the length of the input field and defaults to the length of the column name, OCW is the corresponding Output Character Width used for displaying tables. The POSITION attribute defines the column ordering to be used on displays. INVER-SION specifies whether or not an inverted index is to be maintained for the column.

The TYPE attribute is used to specify the type of data which may be entered into a column. Valid types are CHAR, FIXED, FLOAT, DATE and TIME. IMAGE allows the output format of the data to be defined in an edited form so, for example, a '£' or '$' sign may be included.

The DOMAIN attribute is used to name the set of values from which the data elements in a column are drawn. For example a column containing values representing money could be drawn from a domain called, say, MONEY. Any number of columns from one or more tables can use this domain. For example columns for cost, price, salary, tax and unit-price could all use the domain MONEY. The name entered for the domain attribute defines a new domain. If a suitable domain already exists its name can be entered, in which case the TYPE, IMAGE, ICW and OCW associated with this domain can be used.

The entries in the printed attribute table may be updated in place and then saved. Creation of the table is then complete. The data manipulation operators may be used to actually enter data into the table. Alternatively the Bulk Loader utility may be used to load the table. Tables and domains may also be defined in batch mode using the Bulk Loader.

While the table is being created columns may easily be added and deleted. Once the table contains data no such changes may be made directly. However, columns may be added and deleted by creating a new table, copying the required data using the data manipulation operators, deleting the original table and renaming the new table.

THE APPLICATION PROGRAM INTERFACE

QBE supports a 'linear syntax' which allows the database to be accessed by applications written in the PL/I or APL programming languages. Any operation which may be performed at a visual display terminal can be performed via the linear syntax. The linear syntax simply expresses a query which could be entered at a terminal as a character string. The following example illustrates how a query is transformed into its linear syntax equivalent.

table–name	col1–name	col2–name	col3–name	. . .		
P.		value _LNK	_LNK			

In linear syntax form:

   table–name (col1–name | col2–name | col3–name | . . .)

           (| value | _LNK)

           P. (| _LNK);

The command and condition box entries can similarly be linearised.

The QBE query, in its linear syntax string form, is communicated to QBE from the application as a parameter of PL/I call statements or APL functions. Only the PL/I interface is discussed in order to illustrate its operation. The APL interface is very similar. A preprocessor is not used.

A number of CALLed routines are provided which perform the following functions:

— open the QBE database;

— identify a structure defined in the PL/I program to the QBE system;

— pass the linear syntax query string to QBE for processing;

— determine the number of rows in a query result;

— transfer a specified number of rows generated by a query into the defined PL/I structure;

— provide access to the table definition information;

— close the QBE database.

ACCESS CONTROL

The first level of access control is provided by the VM operating system. Each user has a VM user-id and associated password which defines what that user may do. The facilities available to a user define which database, or databases, may be accessed.

QBE supports two types of database, private database and shared database. The only user who may access a private database is its owner as determined by its user's VM user-id. No other end-users may gain access to such a database. Only the database administrator, who has access to every database, may access the database for maintenance purposes.

A shared database may be accessed by a number of users. However, the user who creates a table in a shared database becomes its owner, As the owner, a user may perform any valid operation on the table. Other users (except of course the database administrator) cannot access a table unless they are authorised to do so by either the owner or the database administrator.

Access authority to tables or parts of tables may be given to all other users of the database or named individuals. The access authorities that may be granted are print, update, delete and insert which correspond to the similarly named language operators. The authority constraints are expressed in a similar form to a normal query. The specified authority applies to the data which would have been printed had the language operator been a print rather than an authority definition. This means that different access authorities can be assigned selectively to the columns of a table. It also means that access can be constrained to rows in the table that satisfy a specified condition.

The example below illustrates how authority constraints are defined. In this example, authority for a user identified by 'userid' is being inserted into the system. This user is being given print authority on part of 'table–name'. Only columns 'col1–name' and 'col3–name' are being made accessible to this user.

In addition, only rows of the table which have 'value' in column 4 will be accessible.

table–name	col1–name	col2–name	col3–name	col4–name
I.AUTH(P.) userid	_X		_Y	value

BACK-UP, RESTART AND RECOVERY

A utility (a CMS Exec) is provided for copying a QBE database to tape in order to produce a security copy. QBE also supports a log file which records all update activity against the database. This log is erased when the back-up utility has successfully executed.

If the database should become damaged the back-up copy may be restored by a utility. A 'recover' utility can then be run to apply the updates recorded on the log to the database. The database tables are recovered to the state at which they were last 'saved'.

Notice that the save command behaves rather like a commit, end of transaction or end of success unit used in other database management systems. Changes are only written to the database when a save command is used. Consequently there is no need for automatic backout to cope with a failed transaction.

In addition to the back-up of the whole database described above it is possible to logically unload and then reload a table. The unloaded copy

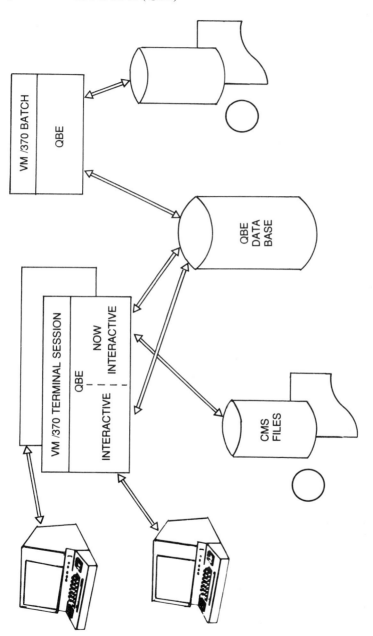

Figure 9.1   QBE Modes of Use

may be used as a back-up. This copy contains all the information needed to redefine the table and load the data into it. The unloaded copy may be reloaded to any QBE database by means of a bulk loader utility.

OPERATING ENVIRONMENT

QBE runs under IBM's Virtual Machine operating system VM/370 and uses the facilities of the Control Program and the Conversational Monitor System. In a virtual machine environment each user logically has the computer to himself. This means that QBE effectively runs in single user mode, each user has his own copy of the QBE code. However, a re-entrant portion of the QBE code may be shared by all users.

QBE is primarily an on-line interactive system for use in conjunction with the 3270, or equivalent, display terminals. Some non-interactive functions, such as a load from VM files can be initiated on-line. QBE may also be used in batch mode by application systems using the PL/I interface and by utility functions. Figure 9.1 illustrates these modes of use.

MULTIPLE USER ACCESS AND LOCKING

QBE allows two types of database to be supported, these are Shared Database and Private Database. A private database, as the name implies, only allows one end user to access the database. This end user is the only person who may create and access the tables in his private database.

A shared database may be accessed by a number of end-users. When the database is simply being read, multiple users may access the tables in the database concurrently. However, only one user at a time may access the database in write mode. If no other user is using the database a user may sign onto it in write mode and gain exclusive use of it for the duration of the terminal session or program. Should the database already be in use by a read mode user then other read mode users may sign on but no write mode user may gain access.

The locking mechanism only operates at the database level. Consequently, concurrent update access to the database is not supported. This means that deadlock situations cannot occur. If a user attempts to sign on to a database in write mode whilst the database is already in use by another user the sign on will fail with an appropriate explanatory message.

10 INGRES

INTRODUCTION

INGRES, the INteractive GRaphics and REtrieval System, is a relational database management system produced by Relational Technology Inc. It runs on the DEC VAX under both the VMS and UNIX operating systems and on Motorola 68000 under UNIX.

INGRES has a high-level language called QUEL which stands for QUEry Language. It may be used on-line and also embedded within application programs. Concurrent update access to an INGRES database is supported with appropriate integrity protection. This protection includes the support of a log. Access to the database, and parts of it, may be controlled.

THE LANGUAGE INTERFACE

INGRES supports a number of language interfaces to a database. The most significant of these is the relational query language QUEL. There is also a version of QUEL for use by application programs called EQUEL which stands for Embedded QUEL.

INGRES also sports a Report Writer, a Query and update By Form facility known as QBF and a VIsual FoRm EDitor called VIFRED. This review concentrates on the features of the QUEL language as a relational calculus language.

The major QUEL data manipulation and data definition commands are summarised in Figure 10.1. Both types of command may be used in a batch or on-line session. Definition of the data is not a separate stage in database creation. The rest of this section illustrates the basic concepts of the QUEL language.

Data Manipulation Commands	
RANGE	defines a variable to substitute for the table name
RETRIEVE	retrieves data from tables based on specified arguments
APPEND	adds rows to a table
REPLACE	updates elements of an existing row (or rows)
DELETE	removes row(s) from a table
Data Definition Commands	
CREATE	defines a new table for the system
COPY	loads a table from a standard disk file
DEFINE INTEGRITY	defines constraints on the data which must be satisfied
DEFINE VIEW	generates a view of one or more tables
DESTROY	deletes a table or view from the database
INDEX	creates a secondary index for a table
MODIFY	allows control over the storage structures of tables

Figure 10.1   QUEL Data Commands

Data Manipulation Commands

RANGE

The RANGE command is used to define a variable name which may be used in place of a table name. If the table name is rather long it provides a convenient way of abbreviating queries. It does however serve a more serious purpose in complex queries. More than one variable name may be assigned to one table. This allows complex queries to specify conditions which different rows within the same table must satisfy for inclusion in the result.

The range variable may be considered to be a pointer, cursor or subscript which references the rows in the table. Sometimes it is necessary to have more than one active at a time.

This command has the form:

RANGE OF variable IS table–name

RETRIEVE

This command is used to retrieve data from a database. The data is normally displayed in tabular form but it is also possible to store the new table generated by the command back into the database thereby creating a new table. The command takes the form:

RETRIEVE (table–name.col1, . . .)

WHERE condition

SORT BY sort–key–id

The simplest form of this command will display the whole table. There is in fact a 'PRINT table–name' command which will produce the same result:

RETRIEVE (table–name.ALL)

Retrieval of data can be made more selective by specifying which columns are to be displayed. Rows can be selected for display by means of the optional WHERE clause which can stipulate a complex logical expression which must be satisfied for a row to be selected. The optional 'SORT BY' clause allows the rows of the resulting table to be displayed in an order defined by one or more columns in either ascending or descending order.

The 'INTO' clause creates a new table in the database which comprises the data identified by the RETRIEVE command. It is used as follows:

RETRIEVE INTO new–table–name (table–name.col1, . . .)

[WHERE condition]

A retrieval request may reference more than one table. In other words tables may be joined. The following query will display the Cartesian product of two tables. RANGE commands are also illustrated.

RANGE OF V1 IS table1–name

RANGE OF V2 IS table2–name

RETRIEVE (V1.ALL, V2.ALL)

The result is a table with rows that are built by concatenating each row of V1 with every row of V2. It will have COUNT (V1) * COUNT (V2) rows, and the same number of columns as in V1 and V2 added together. Of course the result can be restricted by specifying which columns are required and by using a WHERE clause to limit the number of rows to those satisfying a condition:

RETRIEVE (V1.col1, V1.col2, V2.col3, V2.col1)

WHERE V1.col1 = V2.col2

This is in fact the natural join of V1 and V2. Further restrictions on the rows retrieved could have been specified in the WHERE clause. The condition which specifies how the tables are to be joined does not have to be *equality* as illustrated by the example below:

RETRIEVE (V1.col1, V2.col2, V1.col2, V2.col3, V2.col1)

WHERE V2.col1 > V2.col2

Arithmetic statements may be used in a RETRIEVE command in order to generate new columns which are calculated from columns in one, or more, tables. The name used on the left hand side of the expression is used as a column heading when the table is displayed.

RETRIEVE (V1.col1, RESULT = V1.col1*3–V1.col6,
          TOTAL = V1.col1 + V1.col2 + V1.col3)

APPEND

This command allows new rows to be added to a table. It has the form:

APPEND TO table–name (col1–name=value1, col2–name=
value2, ...) WHERE condition

If a column is not assigned a value it will have a null value. The values assigned to columns can be expressed as literals or arithmetic expressions involving other values in the table. The optional WHERE clause is used to identify the row in the table containing the value(s) to be used in the expression.

RANGE OF V IS table–name

APPEND TO table–name (col1–name = literal–value1,

col2–name = 1.3*V.col2–name,
col3–name = 1.7*V.col3–name)

WHERE V.col1–name=value

In this example the new row has its column 2 and column 3 values set to multiples of the corresponding values in a row identified by 'value' in the column 1.

REPLACE

Values in existing rows may be altered by means of this command. It has the form:

REPLACE table–name (column–name=value, ...)

WHERE condition

Only the columns which are being updated need to be listed. As with the APPEND command 'value' may be a literal or an arithmetic expression involving columns in the table. The optional WHERE clause can be used to specify which rows are to be updated. If it is omitted all rows in the table will be altered. The following example increases the values of a column by 10% if a condition is satisfied, it could represent a salary increase for a given grade or department.

RANGE OF T IS table–name

REPLACE T (coln=1.1*T.coln) WHERE T.colm=value

DELETE

Rows are removed from a table by this command. Its format is:

DELETE table–name WHERE condition

The 'condition' identifies which rows are to be deleted. If the WHERE clause is omitted all the rows are deleted.

Data Definition Commands

CREATE

This command defines a new table to the INGRES database.

CREATE table–name(col1–name=datatype,col2–name=
datatype,. . . .)

The names by which the columns are to be known and their default ordering are specified in the list. The type of data that each column will hold is specified along with its size. Character, integer, floating point, date/time and money data types are supported. For example a character string of length 15 is specified as C15.

COPY

A table may be loaded by copying data from an operating system file:

> COPY table–name (col1–name=position–id. . . . .) FROM file–identification

The 'position–id' indicates how the data is to be extracted from the file.

DEFINE INTEGRITY

Integrity constraints may be defined for the data by means of this command. All the data in the database must always satisfy the defined constraints. The command has the form:

> DEFINE INTEGRITY ON table–name
>
> IS condition–on–column–values

The 'condition–on–column–values' clause may specify a range of values that a column may contain. Alternatively, it could be a set of specific values. Cross column checks may also be specified, for example:

> RANGE OF T IS table–name
>
> DEFINE INTEGRITY ON table–name IS
>
> T.col1–'M' OR T.col1 = 'F' AND T.col2 > T.col3

DEFINE VIEW

This command defines a view of one or more tables. A view allows the data stored in the database to be presented to a user in a different way to its defined structure. Data from a number of tables can be presented to a user as if it is actually one table. A view is specified in a similar fashion to a RETRIEVE command.

> DEFINE VIEW view–name (table–name.col1, ...)
>
> WHERE condition

The defined view contains the columns and rows that would be displayed by the corresponding retrieval request.

A view may be queried just as if it were a created table. However, there are restrictions on update operations since it may be difficult to transpose these to the underlying tables unambiguously. Updates should take place against the underlying tables or simple views of them that only reference one table.

Notice that as the operand of a view definition is like that of the retrieve command a view may contain arithmetic statements. This means that a view could translate units, say imperial units into metric units, and include columns generated from other data in the table.

DESTROY

A table definition is deleted from the database by this command:

DESTROY table–name

INDEX and MODIFY

These commands are used to control the physical storage structure used to hold a table. They provide a means of tuning the system in order to optimise performance. Both commands may be used at any time to dynamically restructure the storage structures. The physical storage structures are transparent to data manipulation commands so optimisation can take place without affecting queries.

The MODIFY command is used to change the storage structure. The default is first in, first out. However, other structures include direct and indexed sequential. There are in fact eight possibilities including four which compress the data for storage optimisation. Notice that the default structure could allow duplicate rows whereas the structures requiring a key disallow this possibility.

The INDEX command allows a secondary index to be created for a table. The key may be a combination of up to six columns. Any number of secondary indexes may be maintained automatically for a table.

Other Data Manipulation Features

The QUEL language allows arithmetic operators to form part of a query like many other relational systems. In addition the following mathematical functions are supported:

ABS, MOD, SQRT, SIN, COS, ATAN, LOG and EXP.

Nine string handling functions are also supported, including CONCAT and ASCII, LENGTH, LEFT and LOCATE.

QUEL also provides aggregation and grouping operators which include COUNT, MIN, MAX, SUM and AVG. The functions COUNTU, AVGU and SUMU only operate on unique values, duplicates are ignored. (A COUNTU function is provided because rows in a table do not have to be unique – it depends on the access method used to implement the table). In the example below the sum of coln is produced for each group of rows which have the same value in colm:

> SUM (table–id.coln BY table–id.colm)

The query language also allows selection of rows based on partial string values. For example the 'where' clause: WHERE table–id.coln = "A*" will select all rows which have a character string starting with the letter "A" in coln. It is also possible to select rows which have a character string anywhere within a character string. For example the clause WHERE table–id,coln = "*MA*" will select rows containing "MA" anywhere within the string in coln.

THE APPLICATION PROGRAM INTERFACE

An INGRES database may be accessed from an application program by use of the Embedded QUEL language EQUEL. EQUEL is almost identical to QUEL so statements can be tested on a terminal using QUEL before they are included in a program. A precompiler is used to handle the EQUEL statements. Precompilers are provided for FORTRAN, COBOL, BASIC, PASCAL and 'C'.

OTHER LANGUAGE INTERFACES

INGRES also supports a form-based query and update interface called Query By Forms, or QBF. This is a very easy-to-use system which relies on the user to select the required function from a menu. Users do not need to learn QUEL. QBF displays one row of a table at a time so if a query produces a number of rows the user can step through them.

Another system called the VIsual FoRms EDitor or VIFRED, allows the formats of screens used by QBF to be tailored to individual requirements. It allows the output format of data items to be edited. In addition data validation checks may be established such as range checks, table lookups and even cross-field validation.

A report writer is also supported by INGRES. Reports can be displayed in a default format. Alternatively, a system called Report By Forms, or RBF, can be used to define a complex report structure including break points, sorting, subtotalling, etc.

ACCESS CONTROL

A sophisticated access control facility is provided with INGRES. The first level of protection is managed by the DEC operating system which can restrict access to the INGRES system software. Authorised users of the system can have their access to, and use of, tables strictly controlled. The owner of a table can authorise other users to access it by means of a DEFINE PERMIT command. This command allows the following types of restrictions to be defined:

— the type of data manipulation commands (ie retrieve, append, replace and delete) which may be used against the table;

— the table or the columns within the table which may be referenced;

— optionally, use of the data may be restricted to a named terminal;

— optionally, use of the data may be restricted to a specified period during the day;

— optionally, use of the data may be restricted to specified days;

— optionally, a condition may be specified which limits access to data within the table which satisfies this condition.

The example below illustrates the use of this remarkably powerful and flexible access control facility.

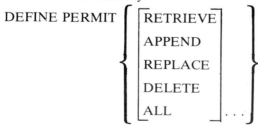

```
DEFINE PERMIT  ⎧ ⎡RETRIEVE⎤    ⎫
               ⎪ ⎢APPEND  ⎥    ⎪
               ⎨ ⎢REPLACE ⎥    ⎬
               ⎪ ⎢DELETE  ⎥    ⎪
               ⎩ ⎣ALL     ⎦ ...⎭
```

OF table–name [column–name list]

TO user–identifier

[AT terminal–id]

[FROM hh:mm TO hh:mm]

[ON day 1 TO day 2]

[WHERE condition]

BACK-UP, RESTART AND RECOVERY

The utilities of the DEC VAX operating system are used to take back-up copies of the INGRES database. In addition a journal is supported which saves updated rows on a second disk. All changes to the database may be logged on the journal, or alternatively the user can opt to journal changes to specified tables. If the database is damaged the back-up copy is restored and then the updated rows are reapplied to the database. This audit trail also allows inspection and selected removal of updates made to the database.

If an update fails to complete for any reason, for example a power cut, the system automatically maintains the integrity of the database by removing partial updates. Each QUEL command is either completed or backed out if a failure occurs. A two-phase commit protocol is used to ensure that either all or no changes resulting from a command are applied to the database.

OPERATING ENVIRONMENT

Each user of the INGRES software has a personal copy of the code. However, as most of the code is re-entrant a number of users may share the same code.

MULTIPLE USER ACCESS AND LOCKING

INGRES supports concurrent update of a database. Locks are used to serialise update activity. These locks can be applied at either a table level or page (disk block) level. The locks are released at the end of a transaction which is usually one QUEL statement but may be a series of commands.

The possibility of deadlocks is avoided by requesting all the affected resources before an update is performed. Update activity is strictly serialised. The lock table used to control multiple user access is held in a data segment within the machine which is accessible to all concurrently running users.

11 ORACLE

INTRODUCTION

ORACLE is a relational database management system which is produced by Relational Software, Inc. It is marketed in the United Kingdom by CACI. The software runs on DEC's PDP and VAX computers under the following operating systems: VMS, RSX, IAS, UNIX and RSTS.

ORACLE supports the SQL relational language. It may be used on-line and a CALL interface is provided for host-language programs. Concurrent update access to a database is supported. A log (journal) provides recovery in the event of the database becoming damaged. A flexible access control facility is also provided.

THE LANGUAGE INTERFACE

The main language interface supported by ORACLE uses SQL, the language developed by IBM for its 'System R' and published in the IBM Journal of Research and Development in 1976. An overview of the facilities of SQL data manipulation and data definition commands is presented in the chapter on IBM's SQL/DS relational database management system.

ORACLE supports operations on tree-structured tables whereas SQL/DS does not. Tree structured tables means that there is a recursive relationship in the table. For example, in a bill of materials application there will be a parts table. Each row will represent a part but some parts are built from other parts. A finished machine (or part) can be broken down into a tree structure of parts where the lowest level leaves represent non-decomposable parts.

A 'START WITH', 'CONNECT BY' and optional 'INCLUDING' clause are used with the SELECT command in order to handle tree structures. The 'START WITH' dictates where the retrieval is to start; it can identify one or more nodes so all leaves below these nodes will be considered. The 'CONNECT BY' clause defines which columns in the table are to be used to link the tree structure. In the bill of materials example this could be part-number and used-on fields. The optional 'INCLUDING' clause specifies a condition that must be satisfied for a lower part of the tree to be included in the query result.

ORACLE's built-in functions exclude null-value occurrences from their evaluations. However, a built-in function called NVL allows default values to be attributed to null fields whenever required.

THE APPLICATION PROGRAM INTERFACE

An ORACLE database may be accessed by any host programming language which supports a CALL facility, for example COBOL, FORTRAN, PL/I and 'C'. Assembler programs may use macros. All the functions of SQL are available to the programmer, there are no restrictions on its use in this mode.

The application interface comprises eleven called routines. These are summarised below. Notice that a preprocessor is not employed.

— LOGON establishes communication between the program and the ORACLE system;

— OPEN connects a program to a database and defines a 'cursor' used to reference an SQL statement active against this database;

— SQL. This call passes the SQL statement to ORACLE for parsing but it is not executed at this time;

— DESCRIBE is used to determine the data types of the fields referenced in a query;

— NAME is used to retrieve the table and column names used in a SELECT clause of an SQL query (this could be useful if the SQL command was read into the application program as data);

— DEFINE informs ORACLE of the location of the data areas in the application program which are used to transfer data between the program and ORACLE. The data type used by the program is specified so that ORACLE can perform any necessary conversion between the internal and external formats;

— BIND allows an SQL statement which has been passed to ORACLE (by the SQL call) to be modified. It enables program values to be assigned to a substitution variable within the SQL statement. This allows repeated execution of an SQL statement with different parameters;

— EXECUTE instructs ORACLE to process the SQL statement passed in the SQL call and optionally modified by BIND calls;

— FETCH actually transfers one row of a result table into the DEFINEd program area. Repeated use of this call allows successive rows to be returned;

— CLOSE indicates that a cursor is no longer in use;

— LOGOFF disconnects the program from ORACLE.

The concept of a 'cursor' allows a number of SQL statements to be active at the same time. Each OPEN defines a cursor. Multiple OPENs allow a number of SQL statements to be active against one or more databases. This enables programs to interleave and nest SQL statements so that, for example, a number of INSERTS, UPDATES and DELETES may be performed for each row returned by a SELECT statement.

OTHER LANGUAGE INTERFACES

The main interactive facility provided with ORACLE is called the User Friendly Interface, or UFI. This allows SQL commands to be executed at a user terminal. In addition to supporting SQL it also supports formatting and editing of results, routeing of output to a terminal or printer, and a comprehensive procedure capability which allows command sequences to be edited, saved and later executed.

ORACLE also has an Interactive Application Facility which is used to define and process interactive applications. An application designer uses the Interactive Application Generator to define screen layouts, data validation rules such as type and range of valid values, and edited display formats. SQL statements are used to access the ORACLE database. Once defined the application is executed under the Interactive Application Processor. IAF provides a means of developing on-line application systems, which use an ORACLE database, easily and quickly. The design may be readily edited if changes are necessary. The generated applications may be run from a variety of terminal types without modification.

A report writer with a text facility is also supported. A report writer utility, called RPT, allows SQL queries to be specified and provides the usual report formatting capabilities such as headings, control breaks etc. RPT is used to access the database and create a file containing a definition of the report formatting and the required database data. This file is used to drive a report formatter, RPF, which produces the formatted report.

ACCESS CONTROL

The access control facilities of ORACLE are very similar to those of SQL/DS. The owner of a table may GRANT and REVOKE privileges to other uses. For further information the reader is referred to the chapter on SQL/DS.

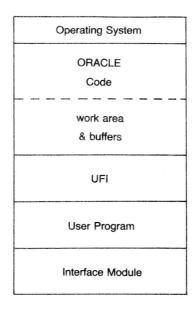

Figure 11.1   ORACLE Operating Environment

BACK-UP, RESTART AND RECOVERY

Standard operating systems utilities are used to take copies of ORACLE databases in order to allow recovery should a database be lost or damaged. In addition ORACLE supports a journal which may be optionally activated for any given database. The journal records after-images, so if a back-up copy of a database is restored the after-images can be applied to bring it back up-to-date.

ORACLE automatically maintains the integrity of databases in the event of system failures. Partial updates are prevented.

OPERATING ENVIRONMENT

ORACLE runs as a task under the appropriate operating system and supports one or more user tasks (Figure 11.1). The ORACLE task includes a shared buffer pool and work areas which are used to transfer data to/from user tasks. The user tasks, which may be on-line users under the User Friendly Interface or batch programs, communicate with the ORACLE task through an interface module.

MULTIPLE USER ACCESS AND LOCKING

ORACLE allows multiple users to access a database in update mode. Locks are used to maintain the integrity of the database. Locking is performed at either the row level by default, or at the table level at the user's instigation.

Commands are normally considered as individual success units. This means that the system assumes that the database is correct after the execution of a command. However, ORACLE supports transactions that are a series of commands which must be complete in order to maintain integrity.

12 RAPPORT

INTRODUCTION

RAPPORT is a database management system which is developed and marketed by Logica. The software is written in a subset of FORTRAN which makes it very portable. All the machine-dependent facilities, such as basic input/output and communications with the operating system, are dealt with in well-defined machine-dependent subroutines. Consequently, RAPPORT is available on a large number of machines. In principal there is no reason why it cannot be installed on any machine which has a standard FORTRAN compiler. It is currently available on the following machines: IBM 370, 4300 series; ICL 1900, 2900 and ME29; Univac 1100 Series; GEC 4000 series; CDC 7600; Burroughs 6700, 7800; Amdahl 470; Data General Nova and Eclipse; Digital PDP, VAX, DEC 10 and 20; Harris 4, 135 and 550; Honeywell 66/60; Magnuson 80; Norsk Data 10, 100; Perkin Elmer 32; Prime 400, 550 and 750; SEL 32; Systime 5000. There is also a 'MICRO RAPPORT' system which can run under most CP/M systems.

RAPPORT supports a high-level data manipulation language which may be used interactively or embedded in FORTRAN, COBOL or CORAL programs. It can support multiple users with controls to prevent conflicts during concurrent update and/or access to the same data. The database is also protected by a back-up and recovery system which includes automatic rollback of failed programs. The system also supports an optional access control facility. These facilities are discussed in more detail in the following sections.

THE LANGUAGE INTERFACES

RAPPORT has a data definition language and a data manipulation language. The data definition language is used to define the logical and physical structure of the database. The data manipulation language consists of high-level commands which can either be used from an on-line terminal or embedded in an application program written in FORTRAN, COBOL or CORAL.

Retrieval Commands	
SEARCH	Retrieves records (rows) which satisfy a set of conditions successively from a file (table)
ORDER ON	Defines the order of retrieval
FETCH	Retrieves a single record
Modification Commands	
SET	Change a value in the record buffer
INSERT	Add a new record (row) to a file (table)
UPDATE	Rewrite a record (row) to the database
STORE	Acts as an INSERT or UPDATE as appropriate
DELETE	Deletes records from a file
Control Commands	
TRANSACT	Defines the start of a success unit
COMMIT	Marks the end of a success unit
BACKOUT	Removes updates performed in the current success unit

Figure 12.1   Major Commands (RAPPORT)

The main features of these two languages are described below. The major manipulation commands are summarised in Figure 12.1.

The Data Manipulation Language

The DML commands can be embedded in an application program or entered at a terminal when the Interactive Query Language is used. There are minor differences in format when the commands are embedded in a program but the philosophy and general form is unchanged. This minor difference in format simply allows a program to receive a status code whereas a terminal would receive a meaningful text message.

SEARCH

The command allows all records (rows) which satisfy a stated set of conditions to be retrieved from a file (table). It returns one record each time it is executed. A SEARCH command must be accompanied by a 'LOOP' or 'ENDSEARCH' statement in on-line mode, or an ENDSEARCH when embedded in a FORTRAN, COBOL or CORAL program. Other statements may be placed between these two statements in order to process the data returned. The command takes the following form:

       SEARCH file–name WHERE (condition [AND/OR condition]...)

       .

       .

       other processing statements

       .

       .

       LOOP (on-line) or ENDSEARCH (batch and on-line)

The 'condition' caters for logical operators involving fields (columns) in the file (table). This command effectively behaves like a read statement which only presents the program with records satisfying the WHERE clause. Searches may be nested in order to access data from more than one file (table) as illustrated below.

       SEARCH file1 WHERE (conditions)
          SEARCH file2 WHERE (file2–field EQ file1–field)

          .

          .

        • processing on selected records

- •

- •

LOOP/ENDSEARCH

LOOP/ENDSEARCH

This example shows a *programmed join* of file1 with file2 on the fields 'file1-field' of file1 and 'file2-field' of file2. A SEARCH command returns records from the database into a buffer; the user has no means of specifying which fields (columns) are to be returned in the SEARCH commands. A 'project' is effectively performed by using the ORDER UNIQUE command and specifying which fields from the returned records are to be written out.

ORDER ON

The records selected by a SEARCH command can be sorted into a specified sequence before being presented to the user or program by using an ORDER ON statement. A sort file is automatically made available to RAPPORT in order to perform the sort. This command must precede the corresponding SEARCH command. It has the following form where 'UP' implies ascending sequence and 'DOWN' implies descending sequence:

ORDER ON file-name BY (field1–name UP, field2–name DOWN,. . .)

'ORDER UNIQUE ON' before a SEARCH command will remove duplicates from field1–name and field2–name thus performing a relational project operation.

FETCH

The FETCH command is used when only one record (row) is to be retrieved. For example if it is being retrieved on its prime key. It has the following format:

FETCH file–name WHERE (condition [AND/OR condition]. . .)

SET

In order to perform an update it is first necessary to change the value of the field being updated. This command changes the field value in the record buffer. In batch programs the records may be changed by direct assignments. The form of the command is

    SET file.field–name := value

where value may be an explicit value, a field–name or an arithmetic expression.

INSERT

This command adds a new record(row) to the file (table).

The record in the file buffer is entered into the database. Every field should be given a value because null values are not supported. Its format is simply

    INSERT file–name

UPDATE

If the record already exists and needs to be rewritten to the database after updating, this command is used. The record in the file buffer is rewritten to the database.

    UPDATE file–name

STORE

This command acts like an INSERT if the record does not already exist. If the record does exist already it behaves like an UPDATE. A message or return code indicates whether it was inserted or updated.

    STORE file–name

DELETE

All, or selected, records in a file (table) may be deleted with this command. Any record which satisfies the WHERE clause is deleted. If no WHERE clause is used then all records in the file will be deleted.

    DELETE file–name WHERE (condition [AND/OR condition]...)

TRANSACT/COMMIT

These statements define the start and end of a success unit. A success unit is a group of statements that must be completed, without any interference from concurrently executing programs, in order to ensure data integrity. Multiple user access is discussed in detail later.

BACKOUT

This command enables a terminal user or programmer to request RAP-PORT to remove all the updates performed within the current success unit, ie since the last COMMIT or the start of the program.

Built-in Functions

RAPPORT also supports a number of commands for calculating summary statistics for all the numerical fields in the records satisfying a given condition. The functions supported are SUM, MIN, MAX, AVG and COUNT. They all have the following form:

SUM file–name (condition [AND/OR condition]. . .)

Notice that all the numeric fields in the file will be summed. It is up to the user or programmer to access the required fields in the file's record buffer. Temporary fields may also be declared so that arithmetic expressions can be calculated using operations +, –, /, *.

Database Definition Language

The data definition language is used to define the logical and physical structure of the RAPPORT database. This definition is held on a Database Definition File which has an entry for each file (table) in the database. A batch processor, the Database Definition Processor (DDP), reads the Database Definition File and creates a Database Common File for initialising RAPPORT's Nucleus.

The structure and format of each file (table) is defined by specifying its file–name and other properties such as number of record slots (rows). This is followed by a definition of each field which specifies its name, type and whether it is (part of) the primary key. Additional indexes may then be specified for individual fields or combinations of fields. Figure 12.2 illustrates the general language structure and use of the language processor.

THE INTERACTIVE QUERY LANGUAGE

The RAPPORT Interactive Query Language allows the database to be queried and updated from an interactive terminal. This language was not designed for use by a novice. It assumes that the user has some knowledge about the structure of the database and tne ability to learn and use its simple programming language.

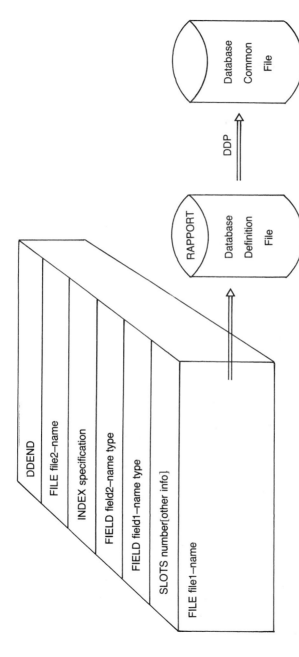

Figure 12.2 Language Structure and Processor Use

The commands described earlier under 'The Data Manipulation Language' may be entered at a terminal. These commands are translated as they are entered but they are only processed when an EXECUTE command is entered. This effectively allows a simple program to be entered and then executed. Notice that each command is not executed immediately it is entered.

The query language supports a HELP command which allows users to display a list of commands and keywords. Command sequences (Macros) may also be stored for later execution. These command sequences support parameters, and prompts for data entry may also be included. A stored command sequence is used by entering its name followed by any required parameters. User supplied functions may also be called.

The IQL has commands for formatting reports such as PAGING, HEADING, FOOTING, NEWPAGE, WIDTH, FORMAT and DATE. A suite of command sequences is available for screen data entry and validation so that casual users may enter data or update the database. Structured programming commands such as IF, THEN, ELSE, ELSIF, ENDIF, WHILE and ENDWHILE allow application programs to be prototyped.

RASQL

RAPPORT also supports a relational query language called RASQL. The main feature of this language is its 'SELECT' command which is based on IBM's SQL/DS. RASQL also supports a comprehensive facility for cataloguing and running queries, including support for parameters. However, the language does not currently support any database updating commands or data definition commands. The RAPPORT database is defined by means of the Database Definition File as described above.

The 'SELECT' command provides all the capability of SQL/DS's SELECT command (see Chapter 8). This includes joining two or more tables, set operations, nested SELECT clauses, data aggregation (GROUP BY, HAVING clauses), sorting (ORDER BY) as well as the standard built-in functions.

THE APPLICATION PROGRAM INTERFACE

The data manipulation language described earlier, with a few minor changes, can be embedded in FORTRAN, COBOL and CORAL programs. The minor changes include the addition of a 'test variable' or status code to a number of the commands, for example the insert command becomes

> INSERT file–name (test variable)

This 'test variable' is used to indicate whether the command was successfully completed or if not to provide an indication of the reason.

The embedded RAPPORT commands are converted into standard FORTRAN, COBOL or CORAL by a Command Processor before the source code is compiled in the normal manner. This processor declares a buffer area in the application program into which the records from the database are read in order to make them accessible to the program. Figure 12.3 illustrates how the processor is used to prepare for execution.

Each execution of a SEARCH or FETCH only returns one record (or possibly no record at all) into the program's buffer area. None of RAPPORT's commands return a collection of records (ie a table with multiple rows).

In addition to the high-level data manipulation commands described earlier there are a number of other commands. These commands include database initialisation, database closedown, a number of database back-up and recovery procedures and access to the execution statistics.

ACCESS CONTROL

An access control facility is supported by the RAPPORT Data Security option which is a 'bolt-on' extra to the basic system. This facility allows access to any intersection of fields and records to be controlled. It also supports data encryption. Access rights are defined by means of a utility, they are not specified as part of the database definition.

The concept of a 'security area' is used to define access rights. A security area identifies a set of rows, based on a field's data value, and the columns in these rows which are restricted. (A security area may be thought of as a view of a table which is password protected.) The file (table) may have numerous security areas defined over it. A password is associated with one, or more, security areas.

The password, which is numeric, defines the type of access permitted to the security area(s). This may be READ or WRITE for unciphered data and DECRYPT or ENCRYPT for ciphered data.

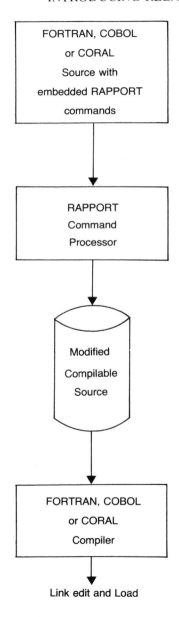

Figure 12.3   Processor Preparation

BACK-UP, RESTART AND RECOVERY

RAPPORT supports a dump facility for taking back-up copies of the entire database on either disk or tape. The single user mode allows the application program to control all back-up and recovery operations via commands. In the multi-user mode the Central Nucleus program must initiate the dump. The dump is only taken at a quiescent point to ensure that the database is in a consistent state. RAPPORT also supports a log file which records before and after images. The after images allow a restored database to be retrieved to a point just before a failure occurred. The before images allow the system to back out a failed transaction. An application program may also ask the system to roll back any updates it may have made since its last commit point. The rollback facilities are also used when a deadlock occurs when multiple users try to access the same data; this is discussed later.

OPERATING ENVIRONMENT

RAPPORT may be executed in either single user or multi-user mode. In the single user mode the RAPPORT Nucleus is called directly by the application program.

The multi-user version of RAPPORT executes in the computer as a

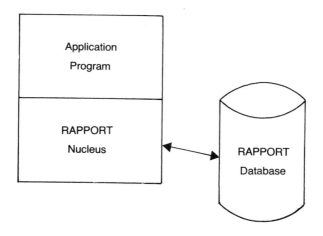

Figure 12.4 RAPPORT Single User Mode

continuously running Nucleus program which waits for database requests from programs, which may be batch or on-line, running elsewhere in the computer. In fact RAPPORT can support programs running in another computer which is coupled to RAPPORT's host machine. The application programs and RAPPORT communicate with one another by passing messages, including data, back and forth by means of the operating system's cross partition/region communication facilities. Each application has a message passing routine associated with it which takes care of the communications with the RAPPORT Nucleus. There is no difference between single and multi-user mode as far as the normal database commands are concerned. Programmers will of course need to be aware of the possible problems of deadlocks which are discussed below.

Figures 12.4 and 12.5 show how the software is organised for single and multiple user use.

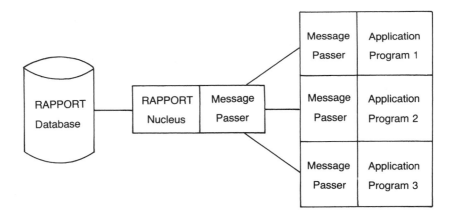

Figure 12.5   RAPPORT Multiple User Mode

MULTIPLE USER ACCESS AND LOCKING

In order to preserve the integrity of the database when it is being accessed by multiple users the RAPPORT system uses a locking mechanism. Two types of locks are used namely 'read lock' and 'write lock'. The read lock for one user allows other users to read the same data but not update it. The write lock prevents other users accessing the data at all. Locking is performed at the record level based on the common property of the records being accessed. For example read locks are based on the retrieval criteria so that all records satisfying the conditions are locked.

RAPPORT also uses the concept of a success unit or transaction. This represents a series of commands that must start with a consistent database, and which end with the database in a consistent state. Success units are particularly valuable where a series of updates are made and all the updates must be successfully completed in order to leave the database in a consistent state. When a success unit is complete all the locks associated with it can be released for other users. In some cases a success unit could be an entire program. TRANSACT and COMMIT statements are used to identify a success unit.

In the event of a deadlock situation occurring, RAPPORT carefully selects one of the affected programs and backs it out to its last success unit thereby removing any updates applied during its current success unit. The backed out program is informed of the system's action via a status code so that it may resume processing in an appropriate manner.

If deadlocks cannot be tolerated, a program may lock all the records it requires in files (tables) before it begins its main processing. Of course such action may also inconvenience other users.

13 Personal Data System (PDS)

INTRODUCTION

The Personal Data System is a relational database management system produced by International Computers Limited. It is available on a number of different ICL computer systems including VME 2900, DME 2900 and ME 29.

PDS commands may be used interactively at a terminal or executed in batch mode. However, there is no interface which allows application programs to access a PDS database. Users usually have a private database but multiple users can concurrently use the same database providing that they are all in read mode. Basic utilities are provided for backing up and restoring a database, however PDS does not support a log so roll back/ forward is not supported. Access may be controlled at the database level.

THE LANGUAGE INTERFACE

The PDS language consists of high level data manipulation and data definition commands. These two types of commands may be intermixed, that is a distinct data definition phase is not required. PDS has been designed for on-line interactive use. However, long-running queries may be run in batch mode by batching together the PDS commands. PDS commands cannot be used within application programs.

Although data manipulation commands and data definition commands may be entered in the same terminal session, it is useful to describe them separately. The major commands available are summarised in Figure 13.1

Data Manipulation Commands	
ADD	add new rows of data to a table
CHANGE	alter (non-identifier) values in rows of data
PUT	adds new rows of data to a table or overwrites existing rows with the same identifiers as appropriate
DELETE	deletes rows of data from a table
LIST	lists the contents of a number of columns for one or more tables
Data Definition Commands	
DEFINE	defines a new table. In addition users' macros and passwords can be defined to the system
DISPLAY	displays the definition of a defined object
RENAME	renames a defined object
REMOVE	deletes a defined object
Control Commands	
STOP	terminates a PDS session
HELP	explains PDS commands
REORGANISE	reorganises a table

Figure 13.1   Major Commands (PDS)

Data Manipulation Commands

ADD

The ADD command is used to insert new rows of data into a table. Its general format is:

ADD list-of-columns [CHECKING rule];

The list-of-columns identifies the columns which are to be entered. If all the columns in the table are to be entered the table name may be used instead. All the columns must come from just one table. In addition all the identifier (or key) columns must be included, as PDS ensures that all rows are unique by means of this identifier. If a value is not specified for a column it is set to null.

The CHECKING rule allows data vetting rules to be associated with the command. A rule may be simple or comprise a number of comparisons linked by 'AND' and 'OR'. Columns in the table may be compared with another column from the same table.

The example below illustrates the dialogue generated by this command:

PDS

ADD   table–name.col1–name,col2–name,col3–name   CHECK-ING table–name. col1–name >100;

XXXXXXXXXXXXXXXXXXXXXXXXXXXXXXXXXXXXXXXXXXXX
TABLE–NAME

COL1–NAME	COL2–NAME	COL3–NAME
< data1 >	< data2 >	< data3 >
< data1' >	< data2' >	< data3' >
< ; >	< >	< >

CHANGE

The CHANGE command closely resembles the ADD command. Its format is:

CHANGE list–of–columns [CHECKING rule];

where list–of–columns and the rule are as described for the ADD command. All the identifier values must be specified in order to identify the row to be changed. A column which is part of the identifier (or key) cannot be updated. The dialogue is similar to that for the ADD command.

PUT

The PUT command behaves just like an ADD if the row does not already exist, as determined by the identifier. If a row with the same identifier does exist it behaves just like a CHANGE. Its format is:

> PUT list–of–columns [CHECKING rule];

DELETE

A row is deleted from a table by means of the DELETE command. All the identifier columns must be specified in order to identify the row to be deleted. If a rule is specified the identifier row is only deleted if the rule is satisfied. The dialogue is similar to the add command so a number of rows may be deleted by listing their identifiers in the table that PDS prompts the user with. This command has the format:

> DELETE list–of–columns [CHECKING rule];

LIST

The LIST command is used to list the data held in one or more tables. In this command the list–of–columns may identify a number of tables, columns of tables or a mixture of both. The checking rule also allows comparisons to be made between columns from different tables. The command format is:

> LIST list–of–columns [CHECKING rule];

This may be used to list an entire table by simply entering:

> LIST table–name;

The number of columns printed may be limited by explicitly naming the columns required:

> LIST table–name.col1–name, col4–name;

A WITH rule may be used to select only rows which satisfy the 'rule' for listing:

> LIST table–name.col1–name, col4–name
>
> WITH col4–name>20 AND col6–name=table2–name.col1'
> –name;

Data from a number of tables may be merged and listed as one result table. In other words two or more tables may be joined. The WITH rule is required as it specifies how any two tables are to be linked together:

> LIST   table1.col1, table2.col3, table3.col8

> WITH   table1.colx = table3.coly
>
> AND   table2.colp = table3.colq;

In this example it is assumed that it is meaningful to join colx with coly and colp with colq. The data in the columns on which the join is performed should come from the same domain.

Built-in Functions

The PDS LIST command supports four arithmetic functions, namely COUNT, MAX, MIN, and TOTAL. The purpose of each of these is clear from its name. Clearly, all of these functions except COUNT, which counts the number of rows in a table, can only operate on numeric fields. They all produce a result comprising one number. All take the form:

> LIST function–name (table–name.col–name);

although the COUNT function may alternatively be used as follows:

> LIST COUNT (table–name);

Data Definition Commands

DEFINE

The DEFINE command is used to define a new table. Its basic format is:

> DEFINE TABLE table–name;

PDS responds to this command by displaying a table which must be filled-in in order to describe the columns that are to form the tables:

> XXXXXXXXXXXXXXXXXXXXXXXXXXXXXXXXXXXXXXXXXX
>
> TABLE   TABLE–NAME
>
> DESCRIPTION
>
> ....
>
> <description – text   >
>
> XXXXXXXXXXXXXXXXXXXXXXXXXXXXXXXXXXXXXXXXXX
>
> COLUMNS   TABLE–NAME
>
> NAME   IDENTIFIER   VALUETYPE   SIZE

\<col1–name\>	\<{ yes / no }\>	\<{ valueset / type }\>	\<size\>
\<col2–name\>	\< — \>	\< ——— \>	\<—\>
\<col3–name\>	\< — \>	\< ——— \>	\<—\>
.			
.			
.			
\< ; \>	\< — \>	\< ——— \>	\<—\>

Each row in the table defines a column name and its attributes. The entry of 'yes' or 'no' under IDENTIFIER determines whether the column is the key or part of a compound key. At least one column must be an identifier and all identifier values must be unique. The VALUETYPE entry defines the type of data which is to be held in the column. The data types supported are INTEGER, DECIMAL, FLOATING, DATE, CEN-TURYDATE (eg 29/05/1950), TIME and CHARACTERS. The 'size' entry specifies the size of the data element.

Different columns in either the same table or in other tables often contain values of the same type and size. In other words the values of a number of columns are drawn from the same domain. PDS recognises this fact and allows 'valuesets' to be defined. A valueset is really a domain definition that specifies the type and size of data elements in the domain. If a valueset with the appropriate characteristics has already been defined it is only necessary to enter its name under VALUETYPE and leave the SIZE entry blank.

A valueset is defined through the following dialogue:

DEFINE   VALUESET   valset–name ;

XXXXXXXXXXXXXXXXXXXXXXXXXXXXXXXX

VALUESET   VALSET–NAME

TYPE   SIZE

....

\<type\>   \<size\>

DISPLAY

This command is used to display the definitions of tables and valuesets. The definition of a named table or valueset may be displayed or, alternatively, every table or valueset in the database may be displayed. The general form of this command is as follows:

$$\text{DISPLAY} \quad \left\{ \begin{array}{c} \text{TABLE} \\ \text{VALUESET} \end{array} \right\} \text{ name ;}$$

$$\text{or} \quad \text{DISPLAY} \quad \text{EVERY} \quad \left\{ \begin{array}{c} \text{TABLE} \\ \text{VALUESET} \end{array} \right\} ;$$

RENAME

RENAME enables the name of a table or valueset to be changed. Its format is:

$$\text{RENAME} \quad \left\{ \begin{array}{c} \text{TABLE} \\ \text{VALUESET} \end{array} \right\} \text{ current–name AS new–name;}$$

REMOVE

An unwanted table or valueset may be deleted from the database by using this command. A valueset may only be removed if there are no table definitions which reference it.

$$\text{REMOVE} \quad \left\{ \begin{array}{c} \text{TABLE} \\ \text{VALUESET} \end{array} \right\} \text{ name ;}$$

Other Language Features

PDS supports a macro facility. This allows the operand of a command to be stored. The macro is used by specifying the macro name as the operand of a command. The stored macro statements are substituted for the macro name before it is executed. Parameters may be used in order to provide a more powerful facility. The macro facility does not allow a series of complete commands to be stored for later execution.

A PDS database cannot be accessed from an application program.

ACCESS CONTROL

In order to access a PDS database a user must 'LOGIN'. The user must provide a valid user-name during the LOGIN process. The database administrator defines the authorised users to the system. There are two classes of users; those who can define tables and valuesets as well as use the tables, and those who may only use tables. The database administrator does not specify a password for a user-name. Instead, the user may define his own password at any time during a terminal session. When the user next uses the system this password must be specified in order to gain access to the database.

Access control is only provided at the database level. Once access to a database is obtained all the tables within it may be used. Individual tables, or parts of tables cannot be secured. This approach is used because the philosophy behind PDS is that a user will usually have his own Personal Database. The system is not intended for use supporting large applications with multiple users.

BACK-UP, RESTART AND RECOVERY

Utilities are provided with PDS for backing up the database and recovering it. If the database should become damaged the latest back-up copy may be restored. However PDS does not maintain a log so the restored copy must be brought up-to-date by resubmitting any changes made since the back-up copy was taken.

The database may become damaged if the system should fail for any reason while the database is being used in update mode. It can also be left in an inconsistent state if a terminal session is not terminated properly when the database is being accessed in 'ALTER' mode.

OPERATING ENVIRONMENT

PDS can only be run in a single user mode so each user has a copy of the PDS software. A single copy of PDS cannot be used to control and monitor access to a database by a number of users.

MULTIPLE USER ACCESS AND LOCKING

The philosophy behind PDS is that each user, or a small group of users, may have a personal database. Different users will normally be using their own private database. However, multiple users may access the same database providing that they are all in read only mode.

A user specifies whether the database is to be used in read only mode or alter mode when he signs on to the system. Exclusive access to the database is required for alter mode. Locking therefore occurs at the database-level. Consequently deadlocks cannot occur. If a user attempts to sign on to a database while another user is using it in alter mode the sign on will be rejected. Similarly, if a user attempts to sign on to a database in alter mode while other users are in read mode the sign on will fail.

Epilogue

At the start of the book we left our entrepreneur discussing relational database with the salesman.

A well designed relational system can be an excellent tool for solving certain problems. It rests on a secure theoretical foundation, but it can only deliver its full potential if properly used.

The database approach – relational or otherwise – needs consistency and commitment from senior corporate management. Database means proper sharing of corporate data, and adequate data administration.

Without these our entrepreneur will continue to suffer from the same old problems.

Further Reading

A good introduction to relational database is given in Chapters 13 and 14 of James Martin's *Computer Data-Base Organisation*, Prentice Hall, 1977.

Another very readable introduction is G Sandbury, A Primer on Relational Database Concepts, *IBM Systems Journal*, Vol 20 No 1 pp 23-39, 1981.

Tony Elbra, *Database for the Small Computer User*, NCC Publications, 1982, provides insight into many aspects of distributed systems.

C J Date, *An Introduction to Database Systems, Volume 1*, Addison Wesley, 1982, is acknowledged as the standard work. It contains lots of examples and detailed literature references. The companion *Volume 2*, 1983, deals with advanced aspects of database systems, including recovery, integrity and data models. Mr Date was one of the first people to recognise the importance of relational database.

Another book is *Relational Database Systems: Analysis and Comparison*, Eds J W Schmidt and M L Brodie, Springer, 1982.

A management overview is given in Relational Database Systems are Here, *EDP Analyser*, October 1982, Vol 20 No 10.

The various suppliers' literature should be consulted for details of actual systems.

Index

References in *italics* are to chapters or sections.